LINCOLN'S
OLD FRIENDS OF
MENARD COUNTY
ILLINOIS

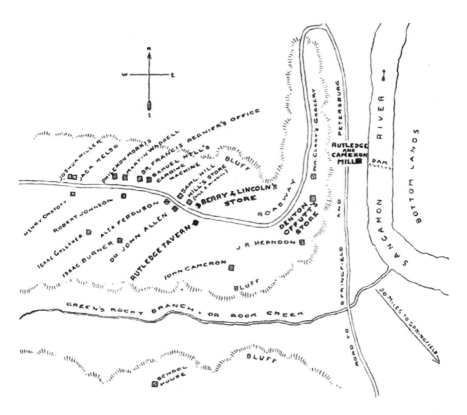

J. McCan Davis of Springfield drew this map of New Salem for *McClure's Magazine* in 1895. He had been studying the deserted site for some time, interviewing former residents and their descendants. By the late 1880s, nothing survived except the buried cellars. The map became a valuable resource during the restoration of New Salem in the 1930s. The farms of Bennett Abell and Bowling Green were located above the map on the Springfield Road. Mentor Graham's farm was on the road to the left of the map. William G. Greene owned the land south of the creek that bears his name.

LINCOLN'S
OLD FRIENDS OF
MENARD COUNTY
— ILLINOIS —

Dale Thomas

FOREWORD *by* MICHAEL BURLINGAME

Charleston   London

THE
History
PRESS

Published by The History Press
Charleston, SC 29403
www.historypress.net

Copyright © 2012 by Dale Thomas
All rights reserved

First published 2012

Manufactured in the United States

ISBN 978.1.60949.797.2

Library of Congress CIP data applied for.

It is truly gratifying to me to learn that while the people of Sangamon have cast me off, my old friends of Menard who have known me longest and best of any, still retain their confidence in me. It would astonish if not amuse, the older citizens of your County who twelve years ago knew me a strange, friendless, uneducated, penniless boy, working on a flat boat—at ten dollars per month to learn that I have been put down as the candidate of pride, wealth, and aristocratic family distinction.

—A. Lincoln, 1843

CONTENTS

FOREWORD

At the age of twenty-two, Abraham Lincoln left his parental home and arrived in the hamlet of New Salem, Illinois, as a "strange, friendless, uneducated, penniless boy" (his own words). He did not remain friendless for long. Among those new friends were Bennett Abell and his wife, the former Elizabeth Owens, both from Kentucky.

In this fine book, Dale Thomas sheds new light on the Abells and their relationship with Lincoln. Elizabeth Abell was especially important in helping the young man adjust to his new circumstances. Though he was notoriously shy around women, he did manage to connect with some of the matrons of New Salem, including Mrs. Abell.

Years after Lincoln died, his political ally and good friend William Butler told an interviewer that Mrs. Abell was "a cultivated woman—very superior to the common run of women about here [in central Illinois]." During his five and a half years in New Salem, Lincoln lived in several different places, including the home of Bowling Green (a cousin of Mrs. Abell's) and his wife, Nancy. While there, Lincoln came to know the Abells, whose cabin was nearby. Mrs. Abell found Lincoln genial and agreeable. In time, Lincoln boarded with the Abells, where he lived "in a sort of home intimacy." William Butler thought "it was from Mrs. Able [sic] he first got his ideas of a higher plane of life—that it was she who gave him the notion that he might improve himself by reading &c."

Stimulated in part by her belief in him, Lincoln became ambitious to make something of himself by studying law. He borrowed books from an attorney in Springfield, twenty miles distant, and read them assiduously in his spare time. Some of his New Salem neighbors were nonplussed by Lincoln's resolute self-education. Before he began preparing himself for a career at the bar, he had seemed a rather happy-go-lucky fellow. Parthena Hill, wife of New Salem's leading merchant, told a journalist, "I don't think Mr. Lincoln was overindustrious...He didn't do much. His living and his clothes cost little. He liked company, and would talk to everybody, and entertain them and himself." Others remembered him "as a 'shiftless' young man, who worked at odd jobs," and as "a sort of loafer."

Lincoln had a powerfully analytical mind and might well have been drawn to lawyers as a class, for they were reputedly the most intelligent members of frontier society and usually owned the largest and best-appointed houses. Lawyers also had an advantage over non-lawyers in the political arena, which Lincoln had entered a year after his arrival in New Salem. Someone who later studied at Lincoln's law office observed that he "took up the law as a means of livelihood, but his heart was in politics," and that he "delighted" and "reveled in it [politics], as a fish does in water, as a bird disports itself on the sustaining air."

Lincoln began his legal studies by wading through Blackstone's *Commentaries*, the work most widely read by aspiring attorneys. Lincoln went at his task industriously, claiming to have mastered forty pages of the *Commentaries* on his first day. He recalled, "I began to read those famous works, and I had plenty of time; for, during the long summer days, when the farmers were busy with their crops, my customers were few and far between. The more I read the more intensely interested I became. Never in my whole life was my mind so thoroughly absorbed. I read until I devoured them."

Lincoln followed a regimen that he would prescribe later to a young man who asked him how to gain "a thorough knowledge of the law." Lincoln replied, "The mode is very simple, though laborious, and tedious. It is only to get the books, and read, and study them carefully. Begin with Blackstone's *Commentaries*, and after reading it carefully through, say twice, take up Chitty's *Pleadings*, Greenleaf's *Evidence*, & Story's *Equity* &c. in succession. Work, work, work, is the main thing."

While studying, Lincoln also held odd jobs, including surveyor. Surveying on the frontier was rugged work, hard on men, equipment and clothes. Surveyors lived outdoors in all conditions while trying to impose order on a wild, untracked land. Lincoln often went to work wearing an old broken straw hat, no coat or vest and pants that barely reached his boot tops. Lincoln lodged with the Abells while he was surveying the hills between New Salem and Petersburg. Mrs. Abell recalled that he often returned at night "ragged and scratch[ed] up with the Bryers." He "would laugh over it and say that was a poore man[']s lot." Trousers often had to be "foxed"—a buckskin cover sewn on the outside of the leg—to save them from total destruction in the brush. Mrs. Abell foxed Lincoln's trousers for him.

Elizabeth Abell helped Lincoln mature in his personal life as well as his professional life. She had observed how brokenhearted he was when his sweetheart, Ann Rutledge, died in 1835. She recalled that "he was staying with us at the time of her death," which "was a great shock to him and I never seen a man mourn for a companion more than he did for her." The "community said he was crazy," but she insisted "he was not crazy," though "he was very disponding a long time."

To help him recover, Mrs. Abell advised that he court her sister, Mary Owens, a well-educated woman from Kentucky who came to visit New Salem. He did so, and the romance went on for a time. Though it eventually fizzled, it helped educate Lincoln in the realm of the heart.

Dale Thomas's book also introduces readers to other important people who befriended Lincoln in New Salem, including Mentor Graham, the schoolmaster who helped educate him; Bowling Green, the jolly justice of the peace who allowed Lincoln to practice law before his court; and Slicky Bill Greene, who clerked with Lincoln at a frontier dry goods store. Making good use of primary sources overlooked by many historians, Thomas helps flesh out the important story of Lincoln's formative years in Menard County.

Michael Burlingame
Chancellor Naomi B. Lynn Distinguished Chair in Lincoln Studies
History Department
College of Liberal Arts and Sciences
University of Illinois–Springfield

ACKNOWLEDGEMENTS

I appreciate the help of those who made this book a reality. Lea Thomas provided the initial resources with her research in family history and also proofread the text and offered suggestions. Professor Michael Burlingame recommended primary sources, read the manuscript and wrote the foreword. Ben Roth and Sandra (Owens) Robert supplied images. Geoffrey and Scot Thomas assisted with their knowledge of computer hardware and software. Kenneth Hodges gave a personal tour of the former Nathaniel Owens plantation. Members of the Green County Historical Society conducted a tour of the old courthouse in Greensburg, Kentucky. John Vineyard and Lou Ann (Owens) Strozyk answered questions about their ancestors.

The gathering of material would have been impossible without the cooperation of the following: Abraham Lincoln Presidential Library; Green County, Kentucky Public Library; Illinois State Archives; Illinois State Historical Library; John Carroll University Library; Kent State University Library; Kentucky Historical Society Library; Lincoln Memorial University Library; Marion County, Kentucky Public Library; Menard County, Illinois Historical Society; Missouri State Archives; New Salem Lincoln League; Oberlin College Library; Platte County, Missouri Historical Society; Sisters of Charity of Nazareth, Kentucky; Washington County, Kentucky Public Library; Western Reserve Historical Society Library; and Weston, Missouri Historical Society.

1
ABELL
Bend in the River

I

Bennett and Elizabeth Abell were second-generation Kentuckians. Her father, Nathaniel Owens, had joined the Virginian militia in 1781 and fought the British-led Indians in the region that became the state of Kentucky in 1792.[1] Owens's future prosperity would be rooted in his military compensation of money and land grants. Robert Abell was the leader of a group of Catholics who left Maryland in 1787 and settled in Nelson County.[2] Robert Abell and Nathaniel Owens met while attending the Court of Quarter Session in Bardstown.[3] They had moved west like their children would, seeking a better life beyond the horizon.

Nathaniel Owens thought Bennett Abell to be unacceptable as a son-in-law. Elizabeth brought upon herself "the displeasure of her father by espousing a man not of his choice; and in point of fact, she was superior in education and refinement to her husband."[4] After their wedding in January 1822, Owens did not go out of his way to financially help them. Six months later, Abell was working as a tenant farmer near Summerville, a mile from his father-in-law's plantation, Lashfield. Although still landless a year later, his personal property had increased from $30 to $1,835 because of the two slaves he now owned. Where did he get the slaves? Perhaps, Owens gave him the slaves as a belated wedding present. Since Abell's relatives in Washington County were slave owners, he might

Bennett Abell's parents were slave-owning Catholics from Maryland. He was born in Washington County, Kentucky, in 1796. His father, Robert Abell, served as a justice of the peace and a representative in Kentucky's first legislature. He attended the state's second constitutional convention in 1799 and supported the article that prohibited restrictions on slavery. Bennett Abell attended St. Thomas Seminary in Kentucky but decided not to become a priest like his older brother. Their mother, Margaret Abell, is buried in St. Thomas Cemetery. After her husband's unexpected death, she blamed herself and took on the life of a penitent. *Courtesy of Ben Roth.*

have inherited them. By 1828, Abell had sold the slaves and purchased a farm near Pittman Creek.[5]

In the spring of 1830, Bennett Abell no longer owned the land he had been farming. The Green County tax book for that year listed him with only a horse and twenty-five dollars of total personal property.[6] Stories were later told in Illinois that he had "married her [Elizabeth Owens] rich, and gotten broken down there [Kentucky], and in consequence had come out here [Illinois]."[7] Buying a farm one year and selling it the next bears some credence to this gossip, unless Bennett Abell sold his land in expectation of leaving Kentucky. Their departure for Illinois might have been delayed because of Elizabeth Abell's pregnancy. She gave birth to Benjamin in July 1830, but he died three months later.[8]

Since the Abells were going to a free state instead of Missouri like his sons, Nathaniel Owens probably cursed the day he enrolled his daughters, Elizabeth and Mary, in Nazareth Academy, located next to St. Thomas Seminary outside Bardstown. In that year of 1814, Elizabeth Owens met Bennett Abell, a seminarian student who decided not to enter the priesthood. Although the Catholic Church owned slaves, many of the

Elizabeth Owens was born in 1804 on her father's tobacco plantation in Kentucky. She met Bennett Abell while attending Nazareth Academy, located adjacent to St. Thomas Seminary. One of the richest planters in Green County, Nathaniel Owens disapproved of his daughter's choice for a husband. Owens served as a county commissioner, sheriff and justice of the peace. He started Brush Creek Academy for his children's education. In the 1820s, he owned over thirty slaves, who labored on his plantation, Lashfield. Brush Baptist Church expelled Owens after he bought his first slave. He later declined an invitation to rejoin the church. *Courtesy of Ben Roth.*

clergy at St. Thomas opposed slavery. They had an obvious influence on Bennett Abell's sense of morality that attracted him to Illinois.

The colors of early fall were already on the trees when the Abells stopped for the last time at Lashfield. Slaves worked in the fields, tending what remained of the tobacco crop. In the laden wagon, the Abells' four children sat among the family's possessions. They ranged in age from nine to three years old: John, Nancy, Samuel and Oliver. Elizabeth Abell probably spoke with some of the slaves she had known since childhood. She said goodbye that day not only to her family but also to slavery in Kentucky.

II

Almost a week after the farewells at Lashfield, the Abells' wagon lumbered into Louisville. They had never seen a city as large, and it probably made them feel uneasy and eager to be on their way. Following the road down to River Street, where teams of slaves were digging a canal to bypass the falls, they found a place for their wagon near the wharf. More than likely, they visited Reverend Robert A. Abell, Bennett's brother, who was starting his second year as resident pastor in the city. Opened for services in 1830, St. Louis Roman Catholic Church had been built through the ceaseless efforts of Reverend Abell.[9]

At sunrise the next day, the Abells waited at the dock as the ferrymen took wagons across the Ohio River. When their turn finally came, the skittish oxen pulled the wagon onto the swaying ferry. Perhaps for the first time reality set in, and as the shore of Indiana came closer and Louisville receded behind them, they reflected on their great journey. For the rest of their lives, time would be measured by the years before or after their removal to Illinois. And like most people who faced a new life in another land, the Abells had the mixed emotions of leaving the place of their births for the unseen future that lay ahead of them. Whatever misgivings, they were excited and hopeful that things would turn out all right for them and their children.

Traveling the dusty roads through the rolling hills of southern Indiana, they saw beneath the wagon wheels black earth instead of Kentucky's rusty-colored soil. As the land became flatter and the trees began to thin out, the strangeness of the prairie opened before them above the yoke of the slow-moving oxen. As far as the eye could see, broken in places by trees along waterways, the tall grass, a rusty red in color, stretched to the far horizon. They crossed the Wabash River at Vincennes, close to where Nathaniel Owens had fought Indians forty-five years earlier. Passing through Lawrenceville, the Abells were now tracing the same trail that the Lincolns had followed the previous March to Decatur, Illinois.[10]

In Illinois, the land seemed even flatter, the grass higher, the days longer and the nights shorter. Now they were impatient for the journey to end, and the children became even more restless and probably began

Covered wagons carried settlers to Illinois in the early 1800s. These pioneers usually traveled in the autumn, when the rivers were fordable and the roads hard and dry. A yoke of oxen pulling a heavy load could lumber along at a mile and a half each hour. To help one another along the way, settlers usually traveled in groups, which often included neighbors and relatives. However, if the numbers were too high, there would not be enough forage for the oxen along the trails of the prairie. *Author's collection.*

to forget their fears of Indians. Except for a few vagrant Kickapoo or Pottawatomie, central Illinois by 1830 was no longer a region where settlers feared for their lives. Native Americans had been forced to surrender Illinois and relocate across the Mississippi River.

Within a week, the weary oxen pulled the Abell wagon up a ridge overlooking the trees along the Sangamon River and near the Lincoln homestead. Thomas Lincoln and his family "settled a new place on the north side of the Sangamon River, at the junction of the timber-land and prairie, about ten miles westerly from Decatur. Here they built a log-cabin…made sufficient of rails to fence ten acres of ground, fenced and broke the ground, and raised a crop of sown corn upon the same year."[11]

A few days later, with the late morning sun behind them, the Abells rode into Springfield. Someone pointed the way to New Salem, twenty miles to the northwest, and the anticipation grew as they pushed on along the winding Havana and Chanderville Road, determined to reach their destination before nightfall. The sun had nearly set behind the trees as they forded a creek, Greene's Rocky Branch, and the oxen struggled up a steep road that led into the small community of New Salem. In the twilight, New Salem seemed to be a meager attempt to bring civilization to the wilderness. Most of the cabins were dark, as though abandoned. Someone showed them the way to the home of Rowan Herndon.[12] The Herndons welcomed their weary cousins, and as night closed in around them, the Abells began to feel less like strangers in a foreign land.

III

With the help of his wife's cousins, the Grahams and Greenes, Bennett Abell cut down walnut trees and built a cabin on the bluff overlooking the Sangamon River, a mile north of New Salem. In the spring, he planned to farm some of the flat, rich bottomland north of his neighbor from Tennessee, Bowling Green. The Preemption Act of 1830 allowed Abell the right to settle on 160 acres without buying the land. In the event that someone tried to purchase the parcel, he had the first option to buy it.

The Abells came to Illinois expecting hardships in the wilderness, but nothing like the weather that hit three months after their arrival. Cranes and wild geese migrated earlier than usual that fall, and the so-called Winter of the Deep Snow struck suddenly on December 20, 1830. A cold rain turned to sleet and snow, although there was a lull at Christmas. Two days before the New Year, a blizzard hit with gale-force winds from the northwest. Building the cabin on a bluff proved to be a mistake since there was no protection from the cold wind blowing in from across the frigid prairie.[13]

The Grahams' homestead was located about a mile to the southwest. When her infant son died, Sarah Graham was too ill to leave the cabin for the burial, and the Abells' six-year-old daughter, Nancy, sat by the fire with her cousin. Trying to survive themselves, the Abells helped the

Grahams whenever possible. On bitterly cold mornings, Bennett Abell burrowed out of his cabin to face another day of survival. Sometimes, while searching for firewood, he found a frozen deer and shared the venison with the Grahams.[14]

The storm lasted for the better part of two months. Averaging four feet, the snow became encrusted with ice after a brief thaw, and then frigid northwest winds plunged morning temperatures to more than twelve degrees below zero. Drifts out on the prairie grew to a depth of fifteen feet. Nearly exterminated, small game and deer, often trapped in the icy snow, died of starvation or were easily killed by wolves and hunters. Famished livestock perished for want of corn, which had to be dug out of frozen shocks beneath the ice and snow. Settlers, snow-bound in their cabins, often had little to eat but pounded meal and boiled corn. If one ventured too far from shelter, there were the dangers of being snow-blinded and frostbitten.[15]

Rural communities like New Salem were isolated, and the mail went undelivered for weeks. The pioneers of Illinois, for years to come, would use this winter as a benchmark of time, and the survivors called themselves "Snow Birds."[16] In late February, temperatures went up, and the thawing snow caused the Sangamon River to flood its banks. According to stories told years afterward, the rivers and creeks "measured higher than they ever had before or since the days of Noah's Flood."[17] The Abell cabin stood well above the high water, but the bottomland to the east that Bennett Abell planned to farm had been inundated, and then rainy weather in the spring further delayed the plowing.

In late April, four men grounded a flatboat on the dam of the New Salem Saw and Grist Mill. Afterward, Lincoln said the locals "might always know when he came to New Salem by the high water the Spring after the Deep Snow that he came down with it as a kind of drift wood."[18] Living close to the dam, the Abells were probably in the crowd that watched as the crew tried to dislodge it. Bill Greene noticed a young man well over six feet tall who "had on a pair of mixed blue jeans pants—a hickory shirt and a Common Chip hat… When I first saw him he was endeavoring to pry the boat over the dam. Whilst straining every nerve to push the boat off the dam Mr.

New Salem owed its birth to a sharp bend in the Sangamon River. At this location in 1829, John M. Camron and James Rutledge constructed a dam and then built the New Salem Saw and Grist Mill. In early spring 1831, heavy rains and thawing snow flooded the banks of the Sangamon. Lincoln was helping to steer Denton Offutt's flatboat down the river when it grounded on the mill dam. In 1940, the Civil Conservation Corps built a replica of the mill and dam on the former western bank of the river, which had changed its course easterly. *Author's collection.*

Lincoln…noticed by his quick river eye the river was falling."[19] One of the crewmen, John Hanks, Lincoln's cousin, helped transfer the goods "from one boat to a borrowed one—bored a hole in the end of the boat over the dam—water ran out and thus we got over."[20]

Owner of the flatboat and cargo Denton Offutt, along with John Johnson, Lincoln's stepbrother, were the other members of the crew. They rested a few days before continuing their voyage down to New Orleans. Making business preparations, Offutt told Lincoln that he was impressed with New Salem's future as a river port.[21] "During this boat enterprise acquaintance with Offutt," Lincoln recalled, "he contracted with him to act as clerk for him, on his return from New Orleans, in charge of a store and mill at New Salem."[22]

In the meantime, Bennett Abell cleared the bottomland near the river and then plowed the virgin soil and planted a crop. "A little corn was grown, and some occasional wheat and potatoes; but aside from these, other grains and vegetables seemed to be little used." Farmers raised livestock since "hay grew abundantly on the high prairies and on the bottom lands...and hogs could almost winter through without the products of manual labor" because of the forage. In the absence of a cash crop due to poor transportation, the agriculture in the region was typically subsistence farming.[23]

The Abells did not have long to wait for somebody who might buy the land out from under them. They had barely started the harvest when Silvestre Baker, who already owned land on the other side of the river, bought another 148 acres in early September 1831. Elizabeth Abell appealed to her father for help; otherwise, her family faced the grim reality of seeing the rich fields below their cabin pass into the hands of someone else. Nathaniel Owens came to the rescue, and the Abells received an early Christmas present. Expecting to be compensated with interest, Owens bought the land and then signed the property over to his son-in-law because of an Illinois law that taxed absentee ownership.[24]

IV

In July 1831, Elizabeth Abell gave birth to another daughter, Mary. At the time, Bennett Abell was one of eight candidates running for the two positions of constable. Henry Sinco, owner of a New Salem grocery, and Jack Armstrong, Bowling Green's half brother, were considered the favorites. Besides the race for constable, two justices of the peace were to be elected, and Bowling Green was among the eight candidates. In addition to local races, voters throughout the state would be choosing a representative to Congress.

The election took place in James Camron's home. The *viva voce* method was used to accommodate the high percentage of illiteracy. Clerks recorded votes given orally, while an election judge shouted the voters' choices for all to hear. By tradition, candidates did not vote for themselves. On the first day of August 1831, John Camron certified that besides the three election judges, "Abraham S. Bergen and Mentor Graham came before me and were sworn legally according to law as clerks of this election."[25]

Bennett Abell and the other candidates, busy soliciting support, voted at the end of the day. In local politics, family ties and friendships often decided who would vote for whom. Elizabeth Abell's uncle Jeremiah Graham and her cousins Bill Greene and Mentor Graham all voted for her husband. However, Felix Greene, another cousin, voted for someone else. Green County Kentuckians Jacob Bale, Levi Summers, James Goldsby and Peter Elmore also voiced their support for Bennett Abell. Among the residents of New Salem, Mentor Graham recorded the votes for Bennett Abell from Dr. Francis Regnier, Reverend John M. Berry, James Rutledge (also running for constable) and Henry Onstot, the village cooper. Although they later became close friends, neither Bennett Abell nor Bowling Green voted for the other.[26]

Recently back from New Orleans, Lincoln walked into Camron's house. Being a stranger in town, he had little idea of which candidates to select. Since Lincoln knew Bowling Green from the previous April, he voted for him and might have taken his friend's advice and voted for Jack Armstrong. His other choice for constable was Henry Sinco; he was possibly hoping for work in the candidate's grocery until Denton Offutt made good on a promise to open a store in New Salem. Lincoln may have been getting on the band wagon for those local candidates who appeared to be the winners. However, he did not vote for the odds-on favorite for Congress, Joseph Duncan, a Jacksonian Democrat.[27] Afterward, he loitered outside the door, meeting the voters of the precinct.

By the time Bennett Abell voted, his chances of winning were slim at best, and Mentor Graham recorded his choices: Duncan for Congress, Robert Conover and Lewis Furgeson for magistrate and T. Hornbuckle and M. Brown for constable. Of these four local candidates, only Conover did not vote for Abell. Instead of voting for James Rutledge, since Rutledge supported him, Abell believed his two choices for constable still had a chance of beating Sinco and Armstrong. But when the day ended, Hornbuckle and Brown finished third and fourth, respectively.

Bennett Abell came in fifth place, with 51 votes out of the 465 cast for constable. Not a very good showing, and yet, for one who was new to the region, the support he did receive made him think about trying again when he would be better known around the precinct. Abell's vote for Duncan, who easily won the precinct and the state, may have been motivated by the great popularity of Andrew Jackson in the region and the difficulty of any supporter of Henry Clay trying to win political office.[28]

2

GREENE

Slicky Bill

I

In September 1802, William G. Greene married Elizabeth Graham, a sister of Mrs. Nathaniel Owens. A few years later, they moved from Kentucky to Overton County, Tennessee. To the south in White County, Greene's aunt Nancy lived with her husband, Robert Armstrong. They had seven sons, including Jack and Hugh Armstrong, and a son from her first marriage, Bowling Green.[29] Rhoda Armstrong, oldest of three daughters, married John Clary before they moved to Illinois in 1819. The Claries were the first settlers in the northern part of Sangamon County, which became Menard County twenty years later.[30] Relatives from Tennessee soon joined them, and the settlement became known as Clary's Grove.

William G. Greene left Tennessee for Sangamon County in 1822. He probably hoped at forty-two years of age that this would be the last long-distance move of his life. After selling his farm, the Greenes' belongings "were packed together in a wagon, and the family, the younger members [Nancy, Francis, William Jr., McNulty, Robert, Elizabeth and Johnson] in the rude conveyance, and the elder boys [Felix and John] trudging along on foot, started on their northward journey."[31]

The Greenes were the pathfinders for their Kentucky relatives, who soon took part in a chain migration to the same region. They settled on a tract three miles east of Clary's Grove. A creek running through the terrain became known as Greene's Rocky Branch. In September 1826, William G. Greene went to the Federal Land Office in Springfield and paid $300 for the 240-acre parcel of land.[32] A mile north of the Greene farm in 1829, James Rutledge and John M. Camron constructed a dam and then a mill at a sharp bend of the Sangamon River. Rutledge and Camron lived on the bluff above their mill. Greene helped to lay out a road through the wooded site that became the village of New Salem.[33]

About the same time, Bowling and Nancy Green settled on a plot of land immediately north of New Salem.[34] William G. Greene's cousin had been a sergeant of volunteers during the War of 1812, and afterward, he married Nancy Potter. Corpulent and jovial, Green became one of the most prominent men in the township, serving a number of years as justice of the peace and leader of the Democrats. From 1826 to 1828, he was a county commissioner, and in 1830, Governor John Reynolds appointed him to the position of canal commissioner.[35]

In August 1829, settlers in the region founded the Salem Baptist Church. Overlooking Greene's Rocky Branch, they built a log meetinghouse near the Greene burial ground.[36] Renamed New Salem Baptist in 1833, the church stood on the property of William G. Greene's eldest son, Felix Grundy Greene, who became one of the preachers.[37] The members were "Hard-Shell" Calvinists, believing only "they were created for Heaven…God made a part of mankind for eternal happiness and the balance for endless misery."[38] Members baptized converts in the Sangamon, while non-believers often stood on the bluff and scornfully interrupted the rituals.

II

On December, 6, 1831, B. Talbott, a county official, "received of William G. Greene six dollars in County Orders for his Tavern License for the term of one year."[39] While his father sold whiskey, Bill Greene worked and boarded with Lincoln at Denton Offutt's store. Lincoln also operated the New Salem Mill, which Offutt had leased from John

After his return from New Orleans, Lincoln worked at odd jobs until Denton Offutt opened a store in September 1831. He clerked and slept in the store while operating the mill that Offutt had leased from Camron and Rutledge. Lincoln became known around New Salem as a pleasant and honest person. Offutt's business ventures were failing when Lincoln volunteered in April 1832 for the Illinois militia. The path on the right leads to the reconstructed New Salem Saw and Grist Mill across Route 97. Clary's store is in the background. *Author's collection.*

Camron and James Rutledge. "Within a few days after the goods were put up in the store at New Salem, I went down there and was employed by Offutt as clerk to keep the store. Mr. Lincoln and I clerked together… and slept on the same cot and when one turned over the other had to do likewise."[40]

Bill Greene thought Lincoln was a "generous" person. His mother was impressed with Lincoln because "he is so accommodating and straightforward [and] he's so honest. She paid him a few cents too much…and he told her of it, and gave it back to her."[41] Mentor Graham frequently dealt with Lincoln in the store: "He was among the best clerks I ever saw. He was attentive to his business—was kind and considerate to his customers and friends and always treated them with great tenderness—kindness and honesty…[He] managed Offutt's whole business. Offutt was an unsteady—noisy—fussy—rattle brained man."[42]

Lincoln had been Offutt's clerk for about three months when Bill Greene came into the store with Richard Yates, a visitor from southern Illinois. (Nine years younger than Lincoln, Yates was governor of Illinois during the Civil War.) "Lincoln [was] stretched out on the cellar door reading Robert Burns, his favorite poet." After closing the store, Lincoln went with them to dinner at the Greene homestead, where "mother had invited some young ladies in…Lincoln was fearfully awkward and timid when girls were around, and I thought he would stumble over everything in the house that day."[43]

Since the rough wooden floor was uneven, chips of wood were put under the table legs. Sitting next to the well-dressed Yates, Lincoln accidentally kicked one of the chips away from the table leg:

> *Directly Lincoln went to reach for something, and withdrawing his arm knocked over his bowl of milk. When he tried to catch the bowl he tipped the table, and the chip being gone, it went down…Yates was at the lowest end, and in a second the milk went pouring into his lap. He jumped up and Lincoln jumped up, blushing to the roots of his hair… My mother tried to make Lincoln easy by taking all the fault on herself, saying that she had no business to set the table where it would bob over in that manner. "Much obliged to you, Aunt Lizzie," said he, "but it's nothing but my blamed awkwardness, and it's no use to apologize for me." "That's you, Abe, sure," replied Aunt Lizzy. "You're ready to comfort a body." "A very good trait," said Richard [Yates], who was both amused and enlightened by the accident.*[44]

Lincoln was the subject of another gossipy story that circulated around the region. Gaines Greene heard rumors about Lincoln and Dr. Jason Duncan's wife, Nancy Burner: "Duncan's wife had a child—father uncertain—supposed to be Duncan's or Lincoln's."[45] He claimed that Bill Greene and Lincoln had "said in my presence that she was a handsome woman—had not much sense—had strong passions—weak will [and] strong desire to please and gratify friends… [They] persuaded Jason Duncan to marry her and move off."[46]

Bill Greene later denied the rumors that were spread by his younger brother: "I knew Jason Duncan well—knew his wife…[She] was a good (clean) girl. Duncan was quite a good physician—practiced in New Salem…Lincoln never touched her in his life. This I know—no man ever touched her. Lincoln and I urged Duncan to marry her and go off."[47]

Most of the women preferred being served by Lincoln and Greene in Offutt's store instead of William Clary's grocery just down the road, where liquor was sold by the glass. The rougher types loitered and caroused there, including the Clary Grove Boys. Wrestling matches and cockfights were the typical means of entertainment. One autumn day, word of an impending wrestling match spread around the community, and a large crowd soon gathered in front of Offutt's store. Offutt had bet Clary that Lincoln could whip Jack Armstrong, the newly elected constable, in a wrestling match. One of the accounts of the contest came from McNulty Greene:

William Clary's store was popular with farmers, who drank whiskey while waiting for the mill to grind their corn. Drunken arguments and fights were common. Gander pulls and cockfights took place outside the door. Women avoided the place and shopped next door at Offutt's store. After challenging him to a wrestling match, Lincoln defeated Jack Armstrong, leader of the Clary Grove Boys. Afterward, they became friends. Identification of the original site of the store resulted from the discovery of its cellar. *Author's collection.*

> *Armstrong after struggling a while with but a prospect of throwing Mr Lincoln broke his holds & caught Mr Lincoln by the legs & they came to the ground. Clary claimed the money & said he would have it or whip Offutt & Lincoln both. Offutt was inclined to yield as there was a score or more of the Clary Grove Boys against him & Mr Lincoln & my brother W.G. Green. But Lincoln said they had not won the money &...although he was opposed to fighting if nothing else would do them he would fight Armstrong, Clary or any of the set. So the money was drawn, and from that day forward the Clary Grove Boys were always his firm friends.*[48]

Bill Greene felt Armstrong had "tried all sorts of tricks, got foul holds and inside leg hitches, all in vain. Then Lincoln said that if they were enemies, he was ready; or friends, as it suited them. Big Jack Armstrong slapped him on the back and said, 'Oh, we were only in fun.'"[49] Disagreeing with his cousin, Mentor Graham believed "no foul or ill play was shown to Lincoln in his wrestle with Jack Armstrong—that it was an ordeal through which all New Comers had to pass. Injustice has been done to the Clary's Grove that was settled by a moral & intelligent set of people."[50]

III

On April 7, 1832, fife and drum announced the spring muster of militiamen around New Salem. According to state law, all free white males from eighteen to forty-five years old had to assemble four times a year, but the regulation was often ignored in favor of a yearly muster. Bill Greene stood in casual formation with his cousins, Bennett Abell and Mentor Graham, beside Lincoln and the other men who were attached to the Thirty-first Illinois Regiment. A militiaman was supposed to "provide himself with a good musket or rifle with proper accoutrements."[51] But these citizen soldiers did not look like a military unit, with "some sitting, some lying, some standing on one foot, some on both—every variety of weapon, the corn-stalk, the umbrella and riding whip predominating."[52]

Nine days later, Governor John Reynolds called for mounted volunteers to reinforce federal troops opposing Black Hawk, chief of the Sauk and Fox Indians. Violating an agreement to stay out of Illinois, Black Hawk had led his braves across the Mississippi River one hundred miles northwest of New Salem. They only wanted to plant corn, but the local militia fired the first shots in what became known as the Black Hawk War. Most of the fighting took place near the northern border of Illinois. If there had been a true emergency in the state, Reynolds could have called up the entire militia of 150,000 men, but the Indians only numbered about 450 braves.[53]

Volunteers to fight Black Hawk eventually totaled around nine thousand militiamen. Most of them intensely hated Native Americans. Less than twenty years earlier, the territorial government of Illinois had given a fifty-dollar bounty for a "hostile" Indian's scalp and only two dollars for a wolf's pelt. "An antipathy since childhood," wrote an Englishman traveling through Illinois, "they should not mind shooting an Indian than a wild cat or raccoon."[54]

Lincoln may have seen the political advantages of being a war veteran since he was considering a run for state representative. "In less than a year," he later wrote, "Offutt's business was failing—had almost failed—when the Black-Hawk war of 1832—broke out." New Salem swelled with "military ardor. Enlistments progressed rapidly."[55]

On April 21, Lincoln, Bill Greene, John Rutledge, Royal Clary, William F. Berry and Jack Armstrong joined the other young men of the region, traveling to Richland and volunteering for thirty days. They were assigned to Company A of the first division of Illinois forces to fight the "British Band" as Black Hawk's warriors were called.[56]

Before leaving New Salem, Bill Greene claimed his father had spoken to the men without Lincoln's knowledge: "There's no question about it, Abe is altogether the best man for captain." They were in agreement, but many of them believed Lincoln was too modest to be a candidate. "Well then, you must keep the matter close, but have a fair understanding among yourselves. Whisper the matter about, so that every vote will be right."[57]

"We will press him into service," Bill Greene said, and then, after the election, he humorously greeted him: "Captain Lincoln, your honor!"

"None of your fun at my expense," Lincoln answered, knowing Greene was kidding and showing respect at the same time.[58] Lincoln later wrote that he "joined a volunteer company, and to his own surprise, was elected captain of it…[And] has not since had any success in life which gave him so much satisfaction."[59]

The New Salem Company rode to Beardstown, joining the other volunteers who awaited orders to move north. "The whole time that I was out," an enlistee from St. Clair County said, "I never witnessed a company drill…I never heard a roll-call in the whole Brigade." He felt like the men were "going on some frivolous holiday excursion, and not to encounter hostile Indians."[60] On the last day of April, they left for Yellow Banks on the Mississippi River. The carnival atmosphere soon turned into a nightmare of cold rain, swollen streams and muddy trails. Motivated by promises of food and whiskey at the end of the journey, the militia found neither as it rode into Yellow Banks on the night of May 3. Hungry volunteers openly cursed Governor Reynolds as they waited two days before riverboats arrived with supplies.

In the meantime, local farmers suffered the foraging of militiamen, unlike Black Hawk's braves who had passed through the region a month earlier. Reynolds's militia met the federal troops at Fort Armstrong on May 7, and the two armies moved northeast from the mouth of Rock River in pursuit of Black Hawk. After the thirty-day enlistment expired, the New Salem Company disbanded, and most of the men returned home without seeing any action. However, Lincoln reenlisted twice as a private, serving until a month before the war ended with the Battle of Bad Axe on August 2, 1832.[61]

Speaking on the floor of Congress in 1848, Lincoln joked about his militia days, in which he had never seen any fighting: "By the way, Mr. Speaker, did you know I am a military Hero? Yes sir; in the days of the Black Hawk war, I fought, bled, and came away…I had a good many bloody struggles with the mosquitoes; and, although I never fainted from loss of blood, I can truly say I was often very hungry."[62]

Some years later, Bill Greene recalled serving in Captain Lincoln's militia company:

> [An] *old Indian came to camp & delivered himself up, showing us an old paper written by Lewis Cass, stating that the Indian was a good &*

true man. Many of the men of the Army said, "we have come out to fight the Indians and by God we intend to do so." Mr. Lincoln in the goodness & kindness and humanity & justice of his nature stood—got between the Indian and the outraged men—saying—"Men this must not be done—he must not be shot and killed by us." Some of the men remarked—"The Indian is a damned Spy." Still Lincoln stood between the Indian & the vengeance of the outraged soldiers…Some of the men said to Mr. Lincoln—"This is cowardly on your part Lincoln." Lincoln remarked, "If any man thinks I am a coward let him test it," rising to an unusual height. One of the Regiment made this reply to Mr. Lincoln's last remarks—"Lincoln—you are larger & heavier than we are." "This you can guard against—Choose your weapons," replied Mr. Lincoln somewhat sourly. This soon put to silence quickly all charges of the cowardice of Lincoln."[63]

Prior to Lincoln saving the Indian's life, Royal Clary said they came upon the scene of a battle that had just taken place: "Whites lost 12 killed—found 11—25 were wounded. They were horribly mangled—heads cut off—hearts taken out—disfigured in every way…[And the] Indians had committed depredations on Fox River—had killed some men, women & children…We saw the scalps they had taken [at the Pottawatomie camp]—scalps of old women & children."[64]

Two weeks before the August election, Lincoln returned to New Salem. "Having lost his horse, near where the town of Janesville, Wisconsin, now stands," Greene recalled, "he went down Rock River to Dixon in a canoe. Thence he crossed the country on foot to Peoria, where he again took canoe to a point on the Illinois River, within forty miles of home. The latter distance he accomplished on foot."[65]

IV

While campaigning, Lincoln stayed with the Abells, whose cousin later took most of the credit for suggesting he enter politics. "Going to send you to the Legislature," Bill Greene supposedly said to Lincoln, who

Bill Greene came to Illinois with his family in 1822. He clerked with Lincoln in Denton Offutt's store, and they served together in the Black Hawk War. After attending Illinois College, he taught for a short time in Kentucky and Tennessee. Returning to Illinois, "Slicky" Greene's shrewd investments made him one of the wealthiest men in the region. President Lincoln appointed him to be a district internal revenue collector in Illinois. Historians believe Greene exaggerated his influence on the young Lincoln. *From* McClure's Magazine.

thought he was joking: "You are crazy, William, and all the rest of you who entertain such a thought. What! Run me, nothing but a strapping boy, against such men of experience and wisdom!"[66] In the end, though, Lincoln agreed, but he was not optimistic about his chances of being successful. "That is impossible. I should not expect to be elected."[67]

On March 15, 1832, the *Sangamo Journal* published Lincoln's statement to the voters of the county: "FELLOW-CITIZENS: Having become a candidate for the honorable office of one of your representatives in the next General Assembly of this state, in accordance with established custom, and the principles of true republicanism, it becomes my duty to make known to you—the people whom I propose to represent—my sentiments with regard to local affairs."[68] He first dealt with the problem of transportation. Railroads being too costly, the Sangamon River should be improved. He addressed the need for usury laws because the chronic shortage of money had led to high rates of interest for loans. Lincoln knew voters were also concerned with improving education. "I can only say that I view it as the most important subject which we as a people can be engaged in." But Lincoln did not suggest any reforms to realize a goal where "everyman may receive at least, a moderate education."[69] Taxes were not popular, and Lincoln knew any public school system would be costly.

A mile north of the Abell farm that summer, Lincoln spoke in the new town, which would soon outgrow and eclipse New Salem. Greene stood in the crowd as Lincoln "addressed the people in the town of Petersburg on the election and the causes which he advocated. It was what the world would call an awkward speech, but it was a powerful one, cutting the center every shot."[70]

On August 6, 1832, the voters of Sangamon County selected four state legislators from the thirteen who were running. Even though the New Salem precinct gave him 277 out of 300 votes cast, Lincoln finished eighth in the county, where he was generally not known. Grateful for the support given him, Lincoln "was now without means and out of business, but was anxious to remain with his friends who had treated him with so much generosity, especially as he had nothing elsewhere to go."[71]

With no means of support, Lincoln thought of becoming a blacksmith, and Bill Greene claimed he caused his friend to have second thoughts: "Any fool could be a blacksmith…Wouldn't you cut a dash, doffing a leathern apron, and blowing the blacksmith's bellows, like another Jake Smutty face, as they used to call Jake Tower…I'll tell you what to do Abe—STUDY LAW; you're just the man for it…You've more brains than half the lawyers in Illinois."[72] According to Greene, Lincoln spoke to him about making the right decision:

> An honest calling and that is the main thing. A lawyer can look more spruce than a son of Vulcan, to be sure; but a blacksmith can be just as upright, if not a little more so…Why don't you know that nearly everybody suspects lawyers of trickery—doing anything for a fee… [and] shielding the meanest culprits as readily as they do the best man…I don't understand why it is that people are determined I shall be a lawyer. As many as ten months ago, two or three people gave me the same advice, though I thought they were half in joke.[73]

Into late summer, Lincoln continued to think about becoming a blacksmith instead of a lawyer since "he could not succeed at that without a better education." Then he had another option. Row Herndon's brother had recently sold his half of their store to William F. Berry, the minister's son. Herndon "offered to sell and did sell" on credit his share to Lincoln and Berry. "Of course they did nothing but get deeper and deeper in debt."[74]

The Lincoln-Berry Store stood on Main Street next to the former home of Peter Lukins, one of the founders of Petersburg. Sometime later, they relocated the store down the street, catty-cornered from X's office and residence. The move occurred because of a business transaction by Bill Greene, who owned the property, the only frame structure in New Salem. Rueben Radford, a merchant, had rented from Greene until the Clary Grove Boys, in a drunken rage, broke into his store one night after a disagreement with the proprietor. Radford wanted out of his business as quickly as possible, and Greene, taking advantage of the situation, "gave $400—for it and they [Lincoln and Berry] gave me $750." Greene went home to tell his father, who had been angry about his son's purchase of Radford's store. "[I] came home and told my father—he said Lizzie get up." Then his mother was ordered to cook "a fust [sic] rate supper" for her son.[75]

Money did not change hands in these financial dealings: "Berry gave his note to James Herndon, Lincoln his to Rowan Herndon, while Lincoln and Berry as a firm, executed their obligation to Greene," who in turn had given his note to another.[76] Greene would soon be called "Slicky Bill" because of his less than ethical business matters, which took advantage even of his friends. Years later, Greene gave his account of the story: "Lincoln and Berry kept the store about 6 or 9 months, and through Berry's negligence and bad management—though not from dishonesty, the store was broken up. A judgment was received against Lincoln and myself on the old Radford note. Lincoln and Berry were to pay this note: it was now Lincoln and Berry's debt. At last I paid it. Lincoln, however, paid me" several years later.[77]

On November 5, 1832, Bill Greene, James Rutledge and Lincoln served as clerks in the New Salem precinct for the presidential election held at the home of Sam Hill.[78] They recorded 185 votes for Andrew Jackson and 70 for Henry Clay. The president also won Sangamon County's and Illinois' electoral votes. Old Hickory was reelected, and Henry of the West, Lincoln's hero, went down to defeat for a second time. In spite of South Carolina's threat to nullify the federal tariff within its boundaries, the major issue was the Bank of the United States, which Jackson was out to destroy. He had already vetoed a bill that would have rechartered the bank in 1836 because it was a privileged institution with too much power over the federal government and the economy.

3
ABELL
Great Friends of Mine

I

Elizabeth Abell first met Lincoln either at Bowling Green's cabin or
when he was clerking in a New Salem store. Lincoln would have been
impressed talking to her since she was unique among the women of New
Salem, who typically came from humble backgrounds with little or no
formal schooling. Her cousin, Row Herndon, thought her to be "a very
smart woman [and] Well educated and was of a Bigg & Welthy [*sic*]
family in Ky."[79] A close friend of Lincoln in Springfield, William Butler,
said she "was a cultivated woman—very superior to the common run of
women about here [and] it was from Mrs. Able [*sic*] he first got his ideas
of a higher plane of life—that it was she who gave him the notion that
he might improve himself by reading &c."[80]

Lincoln soon became a regular around the Abell household. "I
remember hearing my mother [Lizzy Babbitt née Abell] and Aunt Mary
Gill [née Abell] laughing over Lincoln anecdotes, but am not sure they
all happened at my grandfather Abell's. I do know, however, Aunt Mary
Gill said she used to be indignant when A. Lincoln came to stay all night,
for many times she was tucked in at the foot of the bed with one of her
brothers and Mr. Lincoln, and she didn't like it."[81]

Lincoln obviously felt very comfortable with Bennett and Elizabeth
Abell. They were cultured Kentuckians who came from a region twenty

The site of Bennett Abell's farm is south of Petersburg. The Abell cabin once stood near the house on the right side of Route 97. He had originally built his home on a bluff and then later rebuilt it next to the road. Bowling Green's farm would have been to the left of the silo. New Salem State Historic Site is beyond the trees in the background. The cultivated field is adjacent to the Sangamon River. Created by the damming of Bales Branch Creek, Lake Petersburg is above and to the right of the farmhouse. *Author's collection.*

miles from his birth place. At the same time, Lincoln probably looked to them as more than friends, maybe as brother and sister, taking the place of those who had died. And like an older sister, Elizabeth "washed for him and he generally lived in a sort of home intimacy."[82]

Lincoln spent so much time with Elizabeth Abell that gossip began its inevitable journey around the community. Margaret Abell was born in September 1833, and as she grew older, Row Herndon heard a rumor that Elizabeth Abell "has a dauter [*sic*] that is thought to Be Lincolns Child thay [*sic*] favor very much."[83] The village gossips seemed to ignore the fact that Bennett Abell was also long faced and dark haired, besides being tall and lanky like Lincoln. More than likely, the rumor was an expression of country humor. "Jack Armstrong used to plague Abe a great deal about his—Abe's son, which he had by Mrs. Armstrong; it was a joke—plagued Abe terribly."[84]

While Elizabeth gave Lincoln the emotional support of an older sister, her husband provided him with intellectual stimulation. "Mr. Benet Able [*sic*]," Row Herndon recalled, "had a good Lot of history" books.[85] Lincoln borrowed a book written by Amos Blanchard, *American Military Biography*, which contained "the lives, characters, and anecdotes of the officers of the Revolution who were most distinguished in achieving our national independence." Published in Cincinnati in 1825 and 1830, the book included a "biography of Gilbert Motier La Fayett…also, of other officers from foreign countries, commissioned by Congress."[86]

Bennett Abell's collection included another book that Lincoln read, Charles Rollin's *Ancient History*.[87] From 1694 to 1698, Rollin had been rector of the University of Paris and then principal of the College de Beauvais before being forced to retire in 1712 because of his Jansenist views. Originated by Bishop Cornelius Jansenius of Flanders in the early seventeenth century, Jansenism was drawn from the works of St. Augustine. Resembling Calvinism, Jansenism repudiated the Pelagian dogma (salvation by good works and the efficacy of free will) and embraced the doctrine of predestination and divine grace. Jansenism was condemned and censured by the Roman Catholic Church.[88] Completed in 1738, Rollin's *Histoire Anncienne* was a twelve-volume, didactic work that attempted to reconcile classical and Christian beliefs. Greek thinkers had come to the same conclusions as Christians: "Can one behold heaven, and contemplate what passes there, without discerning with all possible evidence, that it is governed by a supreme intelligence?"[89]

While attending St. Thomas Seminary, Bennett first heard about the Jansenian heresy, which may have influenced his decision to not enter the priesthood.[90] He remained a nominal Catholic in a region where no churches of his faith existed.[91] However, he could reason that no one really needed the sacraments of the church since Jansenism, if taken to its logical conclusion, did not require the rituals of a priest. Lincoln would have been intrigued by his friend, a former seminarian, who could converse with him about religion on an intellectual level unlike the few, if any, Baptist ministers or self-proclaimed agnostics in the county. More than likely, Bennett Abell's beliefs and Rollin's books helped to reinforce the evolution of Lincoln's religious philosophy of fatalism and divine grace.[92]

Edward Gibbon's *Decline and Fall of the Roman Empire* was another multi-volume work in the Abell cabin.[93] A convert to Catholicism at age fifteen, Gibbon later returned to Protestantism and then became skeptical of all organized religions. He criticized institutionalized religion and the Catholic Church in particular but never attacked the basic precepts of the Gospel and Christian morality.

During the Civil War, James Matlock Scovel, a press reporter in Washington, frequently met with Lincoln, who on more than one occasion quoted the same lines from Edward Gibbon's *Philosophical Reflections*:

> *A being of the nature of man, endowed with the same faculties, but with a larger measure of existence, would cast down a smile of pity and contempt on the crimes and follies of human ambition, so eager in a narrow space to grasp at a precarious and short-lived enjoyment. It is thus that the experience of history exalts and enlarges the horizon of our intellectual view. In a composition of some days, in a perusal of some hours, six hundred years have rolled away, and the duration of a life or reign is contracted to a fleeting moment. The grave is ever beside the throne; the success of a criminal is almost instantly followed by the loss of his prize, and our immortal reason survives and disdains the sixty phantoms of kings who have passed before our eyes and faintly dwell upon our remembrance.*[94]

Both Lincoln and Bennett Abell no longer attended the churches of their forebears. Lincoln may have shared the same kinds of thoughts with him that he had with James H. Matheny, a clerk in Springfield, during the 1830s: "Mr. Lincoln talked of the miraculous conception, inspiration—revelation—Virgin Mary…His was the language of respect yet it was from the point of ridicule."[95]

Isaac Cogdale, a mutual friend of Lincoln and the Abells, recalled that Lincoln did believe in God and "that nations like individuals were punished for their sins." But he could not imagine a place like "Hell—eternal punishment as the Christians say—his idea was punishment as Educational. He was a Universalist…[and] did not believe in the orthodox theologies of the day."[96] Elizabeth Abell felt Lincoln "was truly a Christian [but] not in the common term now of days [appearing] long face on Sunday and grind the poor on Monday, but he was always doing good the same today and tomorrow."[97]

Bennett Abell had a great deal to tell Lincoln about the Catholic Church and slavery in Kentucky. Emphasizing personal salvation through sacramental ritual, the Catholic Church, avoiding political and social activism, followed a passive position on slavery. At the same time, this was a practical policy dictated by its minority status in American society.[98]

On the contrary, the French-immigrant priest Stephen Badin, whom Bennett Abell had known at St. Thomas, criticized Kentucky Catholics for mistreating slaves and breaking up their families. Traveling about the state, he promoted a fostering of Catholicism among the slaves.[99] Even though he became known as the "Apostle of Kentucky" because of his missionary work throughout the state, Badin's controversial views were met with indifference by his white parishioners.[100] Charles Nerinckx, a priest from Belgium, assisted Badin in this struggle, teaching catechism to slaves and organizing an interracial religious order of twelve young women for ministering to the slaves.[101]

Soon after his ordination in 1818, Robert A. Abell took over Nerinckx's mission.[102] Reverend Abell would later be remembered as "the Patrick Henry of the Kentucky priesthood of the early days…His powerful personality seemed to frighten the governing element in the Church, so he was never allowed to be anything but a poor missionary preacher."[103] He was soon ordered by his superiors to discontinue Nerinckx's policies because of hostility from white parishioners.[104] Unlike his brother, Bennett Abell did not have to answer to a higher authority on the controversy of slavery and the Catholic Church.

Leaving Springfield to assume the presidency in 1861, Lincoln asked his law partner, William H. Herndon, to store his books. Among the volumes were Gibbon's *Decline and Fall of the Roman Empire* and Bishop William Paley's *Natural Theology: Evidences of the Existence of the Attributes of the Deity, Collected from the Appearances of Nature*.[105] Bennett Abell had enough interest in Paley to purchase the book from the estate of Nathaniel Owens.[106]

During their discussions, Bennett Abell and Lincoln may have asked the same question: if God made a universe governed by Natural Law, was not man like the planets destined to follow certain, unalterable, paths? Bennett Abell's exposure to Jansenism at St. Thomas reinforced his musings of a fatalistic universe. Lincoln also had a background of spiritual fatalism from the Predestinarian Baptists.[107] According to Herndon, Lincoln frequently quoted a line from Hamlet: "There's a divinity that shapes our ends, Rough-hew them as we will."[108]

II

Lincoln's bouts of depression were well known around New Salem and likely rooted in the psychological trauma caused by the deaths of his mother and sister. Henry C. Whitney heard that Lincoln's melancholy might have come from a physical problem: "Stuart told me his [Lincoln's] liver did not secrete bile—that he had no natural evacuation of bowels." Whitney believed Lincoln's manic depression was aggravated by this disorder, but the principal cause had been inherited from Nancy Lincoln, which "was part of his nature and could no more be shaken off than he could part with his brains."[109]

Elizabeth Abell did not consider Lincoln a "sad man," but she had seen him "disponding a long time" when Ann Rutledge died. Most of the time, he "was always social and lively and had great aspirations for his friends always decided and good natured."[110] Lincoln frequently visited and stayed with the Abells because he was less depressed in their company. The thought of them moving away from New Salem gave him "the hypo" whenever thinking of the possibility.[111]

Most likely, Bennett Abell, a Thomsonian herbalist, would have attempted to treat Lincoln's constipation. Herbs used as a cathartic grew wild on the prairie or in swampy regions along streams and rivers. Dandelion was one of the milder remedies. Whorlywort, or black root, another perennial, had to be used with extreme caution since it contained leptandrin, a potent cathartic and emetic. The recipe called for a teaspoon of dried root added to a cup of boiling water. After half an hour of steeping, the mixture was divided into three parts and taken before meals.[112]

In Springfield during the 1830s, a "yarb and root" doctor named T.J. Luster advertised in the *Sangamo Journal* that he had cured "sciatic, weak lungs, fits, inward weakness, and nervous affections; liver complaints, fever and ague, pleurisy, asthma, coughs, colds, dyspepsia, rheumatism, cancers, rickets, fever sores, piles, worms and tape worms and many other diseases that affect the human system."[113] A round trip to Springfield took most of the day, and patients sought local treatment without having to pay with hard cash. Herbalists like Bennett Abell probably took payment in kind or did it as a favor.

Dr. John Allen and Dr. Francis Regnier were "regular" doctors in New Salem. Born in Chelsea, Vermont, Allen had a medical degree from Dartmouth Medical School. Regnier came from Marietta, Ohio, where he had a license to practice medicine and surgery. The treatments of these two physicians could be rather severe, and patients were often "purged, bled, blistered, puked, and salivated."[114] It stands to reason that many of the sick preferred the less excruciating regimen of "a certain Dr. Able [*sic*]."[115]

When William F. Berry suffered a severe attack of ague (malaria), Bennett Abell assisted Dr. Allen and others in helping to treat Lincoln's former business partner, who was also consumptive and an alcoholic.[116] Home remedies included a brew of sassafras roots and mullen, as well as a variety of "teas" made from the bark of balsam, yellow birch or white ash and often mixed with wine. Herbalists treated for consumption (tuberculosis) with a number of different remedies, from inhaling the steam of white rosin and beeswax to drinking mixtures of sorrel, ivy, hyssop, hartshorn and beer. Some locals might have suggested wearing a spider around the neck or swallowing one's urine to cure ague and drinking a potion of cider and water gruel or sucking the breast of a "healthy woman" to cure consumption.[117] In spite of their efforts, Berry died from "galloping consumption" on January 10, 1835. Reverend John A. Berry hired Mentor Graham to make the coffin for his son, and on a freezing cold day, the burial took place in the cemetery south of New Salem.[118]

III

During the winter and spring of 1834, Lincoln, "stayed at our house on the bluff when he was surveying all those Hills between us and Petersburg," Elizabeth Abell recalled. "Our oldest boy [John Abell] carryed [sic] the Chain for him…Lincoln would come in at night all ragged and scratched up with the Bryers [sic] he would laugh over it and say that was a poore [sic] man[']s lot [and] I told him to get me a Buck skin and I would fix him so the Bryers would not scratch him [and] he done so and I Foxed his pants for him."[119]

Lincoln enjoyed the company of older, married women like Elizabeth Abell, Hannah Armstrong and Nancy Green.[120] Armstrong and Green could not read or write.[121] Any encouragement to better himself intellectually would more likely have come from Elizabeth Abell. She may have also fulfilled the emotional role he needed after the death of his sister, who would have been close to the same age.[122] She took an interest in his welfare and would soon become a matchmaker on his behalf.

While staying in the Abell cabin, Lincoln decided to again run for the legislature. Without a presidential election, personal popularity again became more important than being a Whig or a Democrat. Another Whig, Bennett Abell thought about running again for constable in 1835. Lincoln announced his candidacy in the *Sangamo Journal* on April 19, 1834, but he did not mention any platform.[123] The Abells' next-door neighbor, Bowling Green, leader of the local Democrats, openly supported Lincoln. Somewhat hesitant to accept the endorsement, Lincoln did not want to compromise his political convictions. On occasions, Lincoln had stayed at the Green homestead and argued minor cases in Green's justice of the peace court.[124]

The election took place in New Salem on August 4, 1834. Since his name does not appear on the list of voters, Lincoln may have been busy elsewhere in the county soliciting last-minute votes. Bennett Abell voted early that day, soon after his wife's uncle, Jeremiah Graham. Both of them voted for Lincoln and John T. Stuart for representative. Later in the day, Mentor Graham and Bowling Green also voted for Lincoln and Stuart. Lincoln received 250 votes, with only 15 opposing him in the precinct. Two staunch Democrats from Kentucky, Zachariah Nance and

James Goldsby, were among those who refused to support him.[125] Of the 13 candidates running in the county for the four seats, Lincoln placed second, with 1,376 of the 8,569 votes cast that day.[126]

Hugh Armstrong, Bowling Green's half brother, voted for Lincoln because he pledged to work in the legislature on a bill dividing the northern part of Sangamon into a new county. John Hill remembered that he had "often heard my Father say that he & many others united Whig & Democrat & got Mr. Lincoln nominated & Elected on the County dividing question."[127] On another major issue, Lincoln supported the building of a canal between New Salem and Beardstown. According to John Potter, "The division was the big question. We elected Abe on the Whig ticket, although the Democrats had a majority. Well, he put our petition in his pocket and didn't do anything for us."[128]

Lincoln's initial venture into the political arena of the Illinois General Assembly amounted to a learning experience more than anything else. Playing follow-the-leader to John T. Stuart, he cast no vote of historical significance.[129] The legislature adjourned the day after Lincoln's twenty-sixth birthday, and he returned to New Salem, determined to become a lawyer. William Berry had died while Lincoln was in Vandalia, leaving him with "his national debt," the responsibility for all the unpaid liability of the failed store that had "winked out."[130]

While Lincoln studied law between his duties as legislator, postmaster and surveyor, he also helped Mentor Graham make coffins. Typhoid, cholera and malaria swept through the region during the hot summer of 1835. Physically and mentally fatigued, Lincoln came down with a high fever. Elizabeth Abell and Sarah Graham nursed him back to health. Five miles north of New Salem in the Sandridge region, Ann Rutledge caught typhoid fever, her condition worsening into late August.[131]

On August 3, 1835, Mentor Graham and Thomas J. Nance recorded votes in the New Salem Tavern. Certifying the election at the end of the day, Bowling Green was again a candidate for justice of the peace. Bennett Abell and Hugh Armstrong, among six candidates, ran for the two constable positions.

Kinship group, religious faith, state origin and personality played major roles in local elections.[132] Except for his Catholic background,

Bennett Abell had a great deal going for him. The Abells were very sociable people, and Elizabeth Abell's relatives seemed to be everywhere around the New Salem region.

Arriving late in the day, Bennett Abell and Lincoln voted for Bowling Green and Thomas Neale, the next county surveyor and Lincoln's new boss. Lincoln chose Hugh Armstrong and Bennett Abell for constable. In keeping with the tradition of not voting for himself, Bennett Abell selected Asa Combs and Armstrong for constable. Among Elizabeth Abell's kin who voted for her husband were Hugh Armstrong, Mentor Graham, Jeremiah Graham and William G. Greene and his sons. As expected, friends and neighbors from Green County, Kentucky, backed him: Thomas and Zachariah Nance, James and Isiah Goldsby, Travis Elmore and Jacob Bale. Bennett Abell also received votes from New Salem merchants and craftsmen with whom he did business: Sam Hill (storekeeper and carding mill owner), Nelson Alley (tavern owner), Martin Waddell (hatter), Henry Onstot (cooper), Robert Johnston (wheelwright and cabinetmaker) and Alexander Ferguson (cobbler). Dr. Francis Regnier and Bowling Green also supported him for constable.[133]

Graham and Nance totaled up the five pages of voters, and to nobody's surprise, Bowling Green was again reelected justice of the peace. Hugh Armstrong and Bennett Abell were elected constable, finishing first and second, respectively, with 127 and 72 votes.[134] Whiskey was usually part of every celebration for those who had not joined the temperance movement. The victorious candidates probably bought the whiskey, and they were toasted as the long mid-summer's day came to an end.

Five days later, Bennett Abell rode into Springfield for the swearing-in ceremony. "The constable was a primary peace officer of the State and was nominally attached to the magistrates court of the precinct [New Salem] in which he was elected."[135] In the prime of life at thirty-nine years of age, he took on a job with duties that "were likely to be hazardous and they required courage and tact."[136] Bennett Abell had to attend grand jury meetings in Springfield. He received a dollar per diem for the nine-day term and six and a quarter cents for each mile of travel. He collected fifty cents whenever making arrests, serving summonses and certifying writs. The types of cases involving a constable included maiming, mayhem, trespass, slander and larceny. Supplied with a copy of *General Statues*, he had to know the state's criminal codes.[137]

IV

Ann Rutledge died on August 25, 1835. At the time, the Rutledge family lived on the Sandridge farm owned by John McNamar, who had competed with his business partner, Sam Hill, for her hand. Soon after Hill bought his share of their New Salem store, McNamar left town for New York to attend to personal business. Ann Rutledge waited for three years, not knowing if she would ever see him again. Sam Hill's future wife, Parthena Nance, knew her because she often "came out to my father's house…Ann did not hear of McNamar for a year…Lincoln took advantage of McNamar['s] absences—courted her—got her confidence

In Oakland Cemetery, Ann Rutledge's grave marker is inscribed with a poem from Edgar Lee Masters's *Spoon River Anthology*: "Out of me unworthy and unknown / …Beloved in life of Abraham Lincoln, / Wedded to him, not through union, / But through separation. / Bloom forever, O Republic, / From the dust of my bosom." Years later, Masters wrote an acrid biography on Lincoln. He refuted the popular tale of Ann Rutledge being Lincoln's only true love, who influenced his life more than any other person. Masters is also buried in Oakland Cemetery. *Author's collection.*

and were engaged. Ann well thought that McNamar was playing off on her." Then she finally received a letter from him "telling her to be ready they having been engaged to be married." Parthena Nance thought "if McNamar had got back from New York before Ann's death that she would have married McNamar."[138]

Elizabeth Bell told a different story: "McNamar returned before the death of Ann [and] McNamar would not marry Ann because she flirted with Lincoln." Apparently, Lincoln and Miss Rutledge had not been on speaking terms at the time she became ill because of the "fly up [at the quilting], but on her deathbed, she sent for Lincoln and all things were reconciled."[139]

According to Mentor Graham, Ann Rutledge "took sick while going to school…She was about 20 years old [with] eyes, blue, large and expressive—fair complexion [and] sandy or light auburn hair." She weighed about 120 to 130 pounds and stood around five foot, four inches with a round face and "outlines beautiful—nervous vital element predominated." Her teeth were good with "mouth well made beautiful [and] medium chin." Graham remembered her to be a "tolerably good scholar in all the common branches including grammar…hearty and vigorous, amiable [and] kind…She dressed plainly, but exceedingly neat, was poor and could not afford rich clothing…[and] was loved [by] everybody. Lincoln and she was [sic] engaged. Lincoln told me so. She intimated to me the same."[140]

Bill Greene agreed with his cousin that Ann Rutledge "accepted the overtures of Lincoln and they were engaged to be married…She was suddenly—a short time before the marriage…sick with brain-fever and died in 4 or 5 days. Lincoln went and saw her during her sickness—just before her death" in late August.[141] Lincoln suffered a severe and prolonged case of depression that alarmed many of his New Salem friends. Either he truly loved Miss Rutledge or her death brought back those dark memories from his Indiana years.[142] Mentor Graham said Lincoln told him "that he felt like committing suicide often, but I told him God [had a] higher purpose. He told me he thought so somehow [but] couldn't tell how. He said that my remarks and others had often done him good."[143]

Elizabeth Abell later wrote that of "the courtship between him and Miss Rutledge, I can say but little." Lincoln had been "staying with us at the time of her death [and] it was a great shock to him and I never seen a man mourn for a companion more then he did for her." One drizzly morning, Lincoln said "that he could not bare [*sic*] the idea of its raining on her Grave [and] that was the time the community said he was crazy [but] he was not crazy…[However] he was very disponding a long time."[144] In the months that followed, Elizabeth Abell's matchmaking led to Lincoln's courtship of Mary Owens; perhaps she hoped her sister could help him overcome his melancholia.

A violent storm hit the region a week before the death of Ann Rutledge. The superstitious in the community might have seen the stormy weather as an omen of things to come: "On the night of the 17th of August," wrote Matthew S. Marsh, a neighbor of the Abells, "a tornado passed over this place, laid the fences flat, rooted up trees, blew down corn and done other damage. The next morn by daylight as I was putting up my fence, two great wolves walked along unconcerned within 50 yards of me."[145]

V

With Lincoln on the verge of becoming a lawyer, his days in New Salem were numbered like the community itself. The town on the bluff overlooking the bend of the Sangamon began to pass into history. Two miles downstream, Petersburg grew in population and soon became the seat for the new county of Menard. Lincoln's post office business had dwindled. On April 9, 1836, Lincoln advertised in the *Sangamo Journal* the names of sixty-four persons who had failed to pick up their mail. (At the time, the receiver of letters paid the postage.) If the mail was not picked up by July 1, "they will be sent to dead letter office."[146] At the end of May, Lincoln closed the New Salem post office and transferred all business to Petersburg.

Observing the sixtieth birthday of the nation, the Fourth of July celebrations included the reading of the Declaration of Independence and the firing of muskets. Taking time out from summer haying, Bennett Abell joined the other farmers, who brought their families into Petersburg

Avard Fairbanks's *The Resolute Lincoln* illustrates the influence New Salem had on the young man. He spent seven years in the village above the bend of the Sangamon River. Lincoln arrived carrying an axe and left carrying a law book. In a 1925 biography, William E. Barton called New Salem "Lincoln's Alma Mater." Lincoln never forgot his old friends of Menard County. Standing next to the Visitors' Center, the statue was a gift in 1954 from the Society of Sons of Utah Pioneers. *Author's collection.*

to hear Lincoln, now running for reelection to the state legislature. The candidates campaigned in a caravan traveling around Sangamon County, an area the size of Rhode Island before being divided into two counties.

Sharing the stump with two other candidates, Lincoln spoke of the policies he had announced in a letter to the editor of the *Sangamo Journal* on June 13, 1836. "I go for sharing the privileges of the government who assist in bearing its burdens. Consequently I go for admitting all whites to the right of suffrage, who pay taxes or bear arms, (by no means excluding females)." After promising to represent all the people of the county, he voiced his support "for distributing the proceeds of the sales of the public lands to the several states to enable our state, in common with others, to dig canals and construct rail roads, without borrowing money and paying interest on it." He closed the letter with a touch of fatalism: "If alive on the first Monday in November, I shall vote for Hugh L. White for President."[147]

Within days of giving birth to another son, Elizabeth Abell may not have heard Lincoln's Petersburg speech. Two weeks later, the Abells joined friends and relatives when Lincoln spoke at a political rally in New Salem. Earlier in the month, Robert Allen, one of Lincoln's Democratic opponents, had talked in New Salem and started a whispering campaign that he was doing Lincoln a favor by not making public evidence that would ruin Lincoln's political career. However, Allen never answered Lincoln's charge that if one "knows of that thing, and conceals it, is a traitor to his country's interest."[148]

On August 1, 1836, Mentor Graham again served as one of the clerks for the New Salem precinct. Along with Bennett Abell, he voted for Lincoln and Ninian Edwards for the state legislature. They also chose John T. Stuart, a Whig, for Congress, and Thomas J. Nance, a Democrat, for county commissioner. Jacob Bale, Thomas Elmore and Joshua Goldsby, all staunch Democrats, refused to vote for Lincoln.[149] It being a presidential election year, Lincoln had less bipartisan support than in the past, but he still did better than any other candidate in the precinct and ended up getting the most votes in the county. Lincoln's future brother-in-law, Ninian Edwards, the aloof, aristocratic Whig from Springfield, also won a seat in the legislature. However, William L. May, a Democrat, defeated Stuart in the race for Congress in the state's third district.

Believing Lincoln to be the perfect mate for her sister, Elizabeth Abell made plans for the second-term legislator and newly licensed lawyer.[150] Parthena (Nance) Hill recalled that "Betsy was a great talker, and sometimes said more than she ought."[151] Lincoln later wrote about Elizabeth Abell's matchmaking:

> *It was in the autumn of 1836, that a married lady of my acquaintance, and who was a great friend of mine, being about to pay a visit to her father and other relatives residing in Kentucky, proposed to me, that on her return she would bring a sister of hers with her, upon condition that I would engage to become her brother-in-law with all convenient dispatch. I, of course, accepted the proposal...I could not have done otherwise, had I really been adverse to it; I was most confoundedly well pleased with the project. I had seen the said sister some three years before, thought her intelligent and agreeable, and saw no good objection to plodding life through hand in hand with her.[152]*

4

OWENS

Of Prairie and Bluegrass

I

An influenza epidemic ravaged parts of Kentucky in 1814, and Nathaniel
Owens lost his wife, Nancy. The following spring, Owens married Mary
Ann Yates, and his daughters, still mourning the loss of their mother,
had difficulty adjusting. Owens always wanted the best education for his
daughters, and now he decided this was the right time to put them in a
boarding school. Elizabeth and Mary Owens felt forlorn and abandoned
in April 1816 when their father enrolled them in Nazareth Academy, a
Catholic school that accepted Protestants. The school was located at St.
Thomas Farm, located fifty miles from Lashville.[153]

A dozen slaves lived and worked at St. Thomas Farm, one of whom,
Ben, frequently ran away. He usually ended up spending a few days in
a Frankfort or Lexington jail. Before going to Mass one wintry Sunday,
the sisters locked him in a barn, but he escaped through a window. Ben
lost a shoe and suffered a frostbitten foot during his four-day ordeal.
After his capture, Sister Josephine took care of him, and the foot did not
have to be amputated.[154]

Bennett Abell and other seminarians studied for the priesthood at
St. Thomas. They were discouraged from socializing with the girls
at Nazareth Academy. The proximity, however, made total isolation

Mary Owens celebrated her first birthday in September 1809. A nanny slave watched over Mary and her older sister, Elizabeth. Lace curtains draped over glass windowpanes. Rugs covered oak floors, and gilded mirrors hung over brick fireplaces with carved cherry wood mantels. Some twenty miles north of Lashfield Plantation, Abraham Lincoln was born seven months earlier in a humble cabin near Hodgenville, Kentucky. They met twenty-four years later in her sister's home outside New Salem, Illinois. More than likely, the photograph dates from the 1850s, when she lived with her husband, Jesse Vineyard, in Platte County, Missouri. *From* McClure's Magazine.

impossible.[155] The Owens sisters may have first met Bennett Abell through his cousin Susan Abell, also a student at the school. She later married Thomas Spalding, kin to Sister Catherine Spalding, the leader of the Nazareth Sisters of Charity.[156] Nazareth Academy moved to the Lapsley farm, located three miles north of Bardstown, in 1822, the same year Elizabeth Owens married Bennett Abell. Mary Owens and her brother, Sam Owens, were witnesses to the ceremony held in the plantation house at Lashfield.

During her years at Nazareth, Mary Owens studied a variety of subjects: reading, writing, grammar, composition, French, natural philosophy, music, logic, rhetoric, history and geography. Her emphasis of study was English literature.[157] She also had to take non-academic subjects: plain sewing, ornamental needlework, embroidery and tapestry work, drawing and painting, health and growth. Supplementing regular school work, Reverend Robert A. Abell, her sister's brother-in-law, and other teachers from St. Joseph's College in Bardstown lectured on chemistry, literature and philosophy.[158]

Nazareth Academy opened at St. Thomas Farm in 1812. Four years later, Nathaniel Owens enrolled his daughters, Elizabeth and Mary, in the boarding school. Conditions were in keeping with the Sisters of Charity's vow of poverty in contrast to the Owens sisters' lifestyle at home. Mary Jane Rowan, one of their classmates, was the daughter of John Rowan, a famous lawyer and later U.S. senator. He built the house in nearby Bardstown that today is known as My Old Kentucky Home. During the Civil War, Lincoln issued an order that Union soldiers must not plunder Nazareth Academy. *Author's collection.*

The idyllic atmosphere of the classroom could not block out the real world. During the summer of the Nazareth Academy move to the Lapsley farm, Denmark Vesey, a free black, attempted to lead a slave rebellion in South Carolina. Before fleeing to Haiti, the rebels planned to execute slave owners. The plot failed, but the news caused panic in the region. Conceivably, Mary Owens read Shakespeare's *The Tempest* and imagined her father enjoying a book in his library while slaves in the tobacco fields plotted to kill him. A deformed slave in the play, Caliban, planned the death of his owner, Prospero:

> *Having first seized his books; or with a log*
> *Batter his skull, or paunch him with a stake*
> *Or cut his wezard with thy knife. Remember,*
> *First to possess his books; for without them*

He's but a sot, as I am, nor hath not
One spirit to command: they all do hate him
As rootedly as I. Burn but his books…

II

Spring at Lashfield contrasted with spring in Illinois. Slaves plowed the rusty, tired soil, unlike the rich, black virgin earth worked by free labor along the Sangamon. Even with the promise of the season, Mary Owens had a vacant feeling in her heart when she thought about Elizabeth Abell not being there to enjoy with her the blossoms in their father's orchards. She imagined the Abells on the open prairie with no trees to tell them of the change in the seasons, but only the wind-swept grass that went on forever under a blinding, cloudless sky. Having never seen the Illinois prairie, Mary Owens knew nothing of the springtime explosion of wild flowers that awakened in the pioneers the same optimism she felt in Kentucky.

After leaving Nazareth, Mary Owens tutored students for James McElroy, the teacher at her father's Brush Creek Academy.[159] The library at Lashfield contained a wealth of books for her to read.[160] Among them, *The Columbia Orator* was a book of readings edited by Caleb Bingham. The author explained in the preface that in "his choice of materials, it has been his object to select such as should inspire the pupil with the ardor of eloquence and the love of virtue."[161] McElroy might have used William Grimshaw's *History of the United States* as a text in the classroom. Lincoln later owned a copy of the book.[162]

In April 1831, McElroy organized the Philo Polemic Literary Society. The group planned to meet once a week in the upstairs classroom of the Owens home. Some of its members were also students who attended the school. "Duties of members consisted of composing, declaiming, debating, and acting dialogues." Any original work would be subjected to formal criticism by the society. McElroy became president and Thomas J. Nance secretary of the society. Eventually, all of the Owens family, including Nathaniel Owens and his wife, became regular members, with the exception of Mary Owens, who was accepted as the only "irregular member." Attendance being mandatory, unexcused absences resulted in a fine. She apparently chose not to commit herself to attending every meeting, evidently a reflection of her independent spirit.[163]

On Friday, May 13, the society debated "whether or not it would be the policy in the United States to abolish slavery by any means." Arguing the affirmative side, McElroy and Nance carried the vote of the membership. Slaves labored in and around the house that day, and the door to the room remained shut. The society's constitution prescribed that meetings were to be secret. However, Nathaniel Owens soon learned of the controversial topic because he became a member two weeks later. Owens almost immediately made a motion that those who placed debate topics and papers in the "Anonymous Box" should have to sign their names. William Skaggs, another slave owner, had previously complained that the box "contained more frivolities than instruction." Owens's motion won by a large majority and discouraged the society from debating topics that should remain unspoken in Kentucky of the 1830s.[164]

Nearly twenty-three years old, Mary Owens might have been embarrassed by one of the debate topics in June: "Which age is the most preferable for a lady to marry, 16 or 20 years of age?" According to the minutes, the question, "after being warmly debated on both sides…was decided by the house 16 votes for the latter and 14 for the former." The following Friday, Nathaniel Owens, who had a slave dungeon in the basement and named his plantation after a scourge, sat in the audience as the society argued the question: "Whether will man go greater lengths from the fear of punishment or from the hopes of reward?" McElroy took the side of reward, and his position was sustained by a vote of fifteen to nine. Before adjournment, the membership elected new officers, and Thomas J. Nance became the next president.[165]

At the second meeting in August, Nathaniel Owens's three daughters were absent without permission. By his request, President Nance "ordered the names of Miss Nancy, Eleanor [Ellen] and Mary Owens to be erased…to which there was no objection." They were supposed to have read their papers on the merits of a "scientific education" for all students. Since a female's formal education at the time did not normally include the sciences, the Owens sisters evidently had little interest in the assigned subject matter.[166]

The second-to-last gathering took place on August 19, 1831. They considered the topic of whether slavery had been "beneficial" to the nation. Thomas J. Nance argued the negative side and won by a large majority.[167] There is no way of telling how Nathaniel Owens voted that day, which came, ironically, during the time of Nat Turner's slave rebellion in Virginia. The news did not reach Green County until later in the month. The bloody uprising cost the lives of 57 whites and 120 slaves. The time for philosophic debate appeared to be over at Lashfield, and the realities of dealing with a large enslaved population crept into the thoughts and fears of white Kentuckians. Owens may have played a dominant role in the demise of a debating society that, in spite of his presence, had again taken on the Peculiar Institution of the South.

While serving as justice of the peace for Green County, Nathaniel Owens presided at this courthouse in Greensburg, Kentucky. At the time, Abraham Lincoln's father was a patroller in adjacent Hardin County. Thomas Lincoln's duties included the lashing of slaves who were found wandering and presumed to be runaways. Returning fugitive slaves to their owners in Green County, Lincoln would have brought them to the jail in Greensburg and conferred with the justice of the peace. Slaves were auctioned and whipped outside the courthouse door. *Author's collection.*

III

Mary Owens needed a cause and not a futile debating society to take up in her idle time. The temperance movement fulfilled two needs for her. She saw it as a worthy crusade that allowed her to spend time with Thomas J. Nance. In 1826, the American Temperance Society was founded in Boston, and local groups followed within a couple of years. Members crusaded to get temperance pledges out of those who indulged in the drinking of spirits. The call for moderate drinking soon led to demands for total abstinence from many of the organizations. New York, Michigan, Iowa and New England had passed prohibition laws by the 1850s. Local option became the law in Illinois and Missouri; other states, like Kentucky, had no prohibition laws. Founded in 1830, Lexington had the first temperance society in Kentucky. Twelve years later, thirty thousand pledges in the state swore off alcoholic beverages. At a time when women played a limited role outside the home, the temperance movement gave them the opportunity to get involved politically for the first time.[168]

Mary Owens probably first heard about the evils of whiskey from sermons in Brush Baptist Church, although the sect later split over the controversy. Calvinism among Baptists had evolved by the nineteenth century to include all those who were faithful members of the church. They were all God's elect and predestined for heaven. Sensual over-indulgence corrupted the elect, and liquor was often to blame. The typical temperance society had female membership ranging from 35 to 60 percent. *Godey's Lady's Book*, a popular magazine first published in 1830, won converts to temperance with prose and poetry: "He braved the snow. He faced the storm / And journeyed o'er the plain / But never to his wife and child / The drunkard came again."[169]

In the Owens library, Dr. Samuel Johnson's *A Dictionary of the English Language* contained over forty thousand definitions with quotations from famous writers to illustrate the words. For a young woman looking for a cause to join, Mary Owens would have been impressed with one of Johnson's wittier definitions: "Distiller: One who makes and sells pernicious and inflammatory spirits."[170] In spite of her father distilling his corn into whiskey, she became a member of the temperance movement.

On the Fourth of July 1832, Mary Owens listened to an address given by Thomas J. Nance. At the close of his speech, he turned to his support of the temperance movement: "[S]ociety is much injured and depraved by the corrupting influence of the bottle." Besides the subject at hand, he also may have been thinking of slavery when saying that "if the use or exercise of any privilege causes more evil than good, it should be considered as an act of wisdom to quit its practice." Looking at the women in the audience, Nance probably made Mary Owens's heart throb with emotion when he closed his speech: "With confidence we refer the interest of the Temperance Cause to the fair sex, whose generous feelings are ever ready to alleviate our cares; whose influence in society is to my opinion much under-rated. Your tender nature, your love of domestic and social enjoyment and attractive graces and prospects in life all invite your attention, and friendly aid."[171]

In early October, the Nance family planned to leave slavery behind them and settle in the free state of Illinois. In spite of their differences over the matter of slavery, Nathaniel Owens wrote a letter about the Nances that sounded like a character reference:

> *Mr. Zachariah Nance and his wife have been near neighbors to me for twenty six years. They have been respectable, good neighbors. I regret that I must part with them…Their children now go with them, to wit, Thomas, Allen and Parthena who was born in the house they now go from and have my best wishes for their prosperity. Mr. Thomas Nance has approached manhood and has been doing business for his father the last 12 months.…Not one of the family know of my intention of giving this certificate nor will they know it until I hand it to them. I write for my satisfaction and to stimulate them to remember their old neighbor.*[172]

IV

In October 1833, Mary Owens planned to visit her sister in Illinois. She had just celebrated her twenty-fifth birthday, two weeks after her younger sister, Nancy, married John W. Vineyard. Another marriage at Lashfield was planned for November when yet another younger sister, Ellen, would marry Albert G. Williams. Perhaps she felt the need to get away from the whispers of her approaching spinsterhood. "Letters from Betsey [Abell] encouraged Mary to visit, and Mary prevailed on her father to let her go see Betsey and family. The journey from Kentucky to Illinois was carefully planned. Neighbors nearby were going to New Salem and Mary would be safe and properly chaperoned."[173] More than likely, she made the journey with John W. Vineyard and Albert C. Williams, who had business interests in Sangamon County.

Mary Owens had not seen the Abells for three years and the Grahams for five years. She renewed acquaintances with Parthena Nance, now living with her parents at Farmers' Point, two miles south of New Salem. Also, she wanted to again see Thomas J. Nance. Sometime later, Mary Owens wrote him a puzzling letter about their relationship:

> *My feelings at the moment, felt deeply, and I determined, as you had set the example, to profit from it, but we are commanded to do good for evil, and in this particular, I am resolved to obey the injunction…Wherein consists the impropriety of my corresponding with an absent Friend, and admiting [sic] at the same time, that Friend to be a Gentleman. We are beings formed for social intercourse, and I hold it admissable [sic] for us, to draw pleasure from what ever source we can, provided, it be an innocent one.*[174]

She saw another former Kentuckian during the four-week stay with her sister: "Lincoln was a frequent visitor at the house of Able [sic] and a warm friend of the family, and during the first visit of Mary Owens, which did not continue a great while, he learned to admire her very much…She was light-hearted and cheery in her disposition. She was kind and considerate for those, with whom she was thrown in contact."[175] At the time, Lincoln boarded in the Rutledge Tavern. He would have been impressed with her knowledge of English literature. Mary Owens "was a good conversationalist and a splendid reader, but very few persons being found to equal her in this accomplishment."[176]

Considering his nervousness in the company of Mary Owens, Lincoln's behavior, as told in a Green County, Kentucky tale, may not necessarily be apocryphal: "Lincoln was fond of jam and when the preserve stand was passed around, he took a hearty helping. [But his] portion of jam seemed to have unusual body; a few passes with his knife disclosed the reason." A day or two earlier, perhaps one of the children snacking had failed to put the top back on the preserve stand. "The jam had lured an inquisitive and hungry mouse…whose rather unappetizing remains lay entombed in the preserve stand until it was unexpectedly liberated by Lincoln." Not wanting to offend the Abells or embarrass Miss Owens, "Lincoln was in a quandary. He had expressed his fondness for jam, and if he left his portion on his plate, it would excite inquiry and examination." With nowhere to hide the mouse, "Lincoln took one last look at the lump on his plate—then he ate it."[177]

V

Mary Owens returned to Kentucky, a state in transition during the 1830s. The number of slaves had peaked and would begin a decline in the next decade. Smaller yields caused by the overplanting of tobacco reduced the demand for slaves. Kentuckians who moved to Missouri usually took their slaves with them. Some were sold downriver in the lower South because of the higher auction prices. Nathaniel Owens remained one of the more prominent citizens of the county and continued to operate Brush Creek Academy in his home. Unwed at age twenty-eight, Mary Owens worried her father. She had entertained suitors, but apparently she saw none of them as worthy of her hand.

In April 1835, Mary Owens reproached Thomas J. Nance for not mentioning her name in letters he had sent to Jefferson Henry, a mutual friend:

> *You are aware Thomas, that in writing you this letter, I am transgressing the circumscribed limits, laid down by tyrannical custom, for our sex. But why should I not indulge in this harmless gratification, prompted by feelings of friendship?…Then, if I am condemned by the cold, unfeeling and fastidious of either Sex, I care not, for I trust, my Heart,*

has learned to rise superior to those groveling feelings, dictated by bosoms, that are callous to every refined emotion. I am much pleased to learn, that you intend visiting Green [County] this spring, for my own part, I frankly say, (without the slightest tinge of flattery) that you have many Friends here, whose Hearts beat high, at the thought of seeing you again, for my part, I frankly acknowledge, that to me, it would be a treat of no every day occurence [sic], to see Thomas, and talk about days of Auld Lang Sine. [178]

Nance's recent marriage to Catherine Houghton of Rock Creek, Illinois, probably made Mary Owens feel that life was passing her by at an even greater pace. She self-mockingly referred to herself as being in "Rural Retirement, Green Cty Ky." Then she went on to describe the people around her as though an observer instead of a direct participant in life:

I know of no recent changes among your acquaintances, except the Marriage of Mr. Thomas Henry, to Miss Certly, a Cousin of his. Jefferson is still single, retaining as much life and vivacity as ever. I saw Sam Sympson a few Days since, he was well, and speaks of visiting your state, perhaps this fall. Irvin will leave Green [County] in a short time for Missouri, but says he intends returning in May, the opinion I believe, generally prevails, that Miss White, a sister of Daniels, is the attraction which draws him back. Nancy and Ellen [her married sisters] are here, and will not leave until Fall, at which time they contemplate on moving to Illinois. [179]

VI

In autumn 1836, Elizabeth Abell came back to Lashfield for the first time in six years. Besides the desire to again see her family, she had a plan to act as a matchmaker for Lincoln and her sister. Mary Owens received advance notice from Parthena, who had recently married Sam Hill. "Lincoln had boasted that he would marry Miss Owens if she came a second time to Illinois…She left her Kentucky home with a predetermination to show him, if she met him, that she was not to be caught simply by the asking."[180]

Nathaniel Owens probably looked upon the match with mixed feelings. Although a lawyer and a Whig in the Illinois General Assembly, Lincoln could barely support himself, let alone a wife. Elizabeth Abell spoke for his character, and her father had known members of the Lincoln family in Kentucky. The Lincolns were anti-slave but not Abolitionists. On the day he said goodbye to his daughters, Owens might have thought that having Lincoln as a son-in-law was not the worst thing in the world.

The sisters went by steamboat down the Ohio and then up the Mississippi and Illinois Rivers to Havana, Illinois. The last leg of their long journey would be a stagecoach ride of twenty-five miles to New

New Salem State Historic Site recalls the past when man depended on horses for transportation. In the nineteenth century, this scene would have been common throughout Menard County. Farmers grew crops to feed humans and livestock, including horses. County seats were normally located where the farthest traveler could by horse make a round trip in the same day. Stealing another man's horse was considered a capital crime on the western frontier. Even today, automobile engines are rated according to horsepower. *Author's collection.*

Salem.[181] In the dewy mist of early morning, they left the river town. The sun rose above the horizon in the direction of their destination. The stagecoach made its way along the bumpy road that divided the flat fields with the stubble of harvest. The few trees along the route were leafless. About noon, they passed beneath the Abell cabin on the bluff, and the stagecoach went up the hill into New Salem, stopping in front of the tavern. Being an election day, the hamlet was busier then usual for a Tuesday in November.

5

GRAHAM

Schoolmaster

I

Mentor Graham's grandparents, William Graham and Nancy Graham (née Lynn), were the connecting link of the three families (Abell, Greene and Graham) who settled outside New Salem, Illinois. After suffering financial setbacks in Kentucky, Mentor Graham brought his family to the region in the autumn of 1826. He had been a student and then a teacher at his uncle's Brush Creek Academy. Graham served as headmaster at Greensburg Academy, his last teaching position in Kentucky.

Starting over again at the age of twenty-six years, Mentor Graham settled on forty acres located a quarter of a mile west of the future site of New Salem. He put up a makeshift cabin but in the mid-1830s built the first brick house in the region. Besides farming and brick making, Graham taught school until 1838 in the Baptist church located on the farm of his cousin Felix Greene, just outside New Salem.[182] As a result of the scarcity of money, Graham often received tuition in the form of eggs, butter, corn, venison or whatever else the parents had to barter. Graham's students included children of a number of families: Abell, Greene, Rutledge, Armstrong, Bale, Cameron, Potter, Barbee and Sampson.[183] Graham also tutored students in their homes.

In keeping with the teaching methods of the times, Graham's students were expected to memorize endless lessons and "blab" them out on

In late autumn 1800, William Mentor Graham was born in a small cabin built by his father, Jeremiah Graham, eight miles west of Greensburg, Kentucky. Mentor Graham attended Brush Creek Academy, where he later taught classes. He married Sarah Rafferty, and they settled on a small farm near his birthplace. To supplement the family income, he did some surveying, which he had learned from Uncle Nathaniel Owens. Graham also peddled books door-to-door and made bricks when he was not teaching or farming. *From* McClure's Magazine.

command. "He always kept a lot of good switches on hand…often calling up a scholar and make him hold out his hand and with his rule, lay on the licks until the scholar would beg for mercy."[184] The younger brother of Ann Rutledge, Robert B. Rutledge, had fond memories of Graham: "I remember my old teacher with gratitude. Place him in his true light, before the reading world, and award to him that need of praise that is due the man, who assisted in laying the foundation of Mr. Lincoln's greatness. I know of my own knowledge that Mr. Graham contributed more to Mr. L.['s] education whilst in New Salem than any other man."[185]

Mentor Graham was more conventional about religion than Bennett Abell. He became like his cousin another sounding board for Lincoln's questions: "Lincoln was living at my house at New Salem…in the year 1833. One morning he said to me, 'Graham, what do you think about the anger of the Lord?' I replied, 'I believe the Lord never was angry or mad and never would be; that his loving-kindness endureth forever; that he never changes.'" Lincoln showed him a manuscript "on the subject of Christianity and a defense of universal salvation," which he thought of publishing. Graham believed Lincoln's reasoning rivaled any book he

In the 1930s, the Civil Conservation Corps rebuilt the New Salem Schoolhouse near the original site across Greene's Rocky Branch. Mentor Graham held classes here from 1829 to 1838. The primitive conditions were typical of the settlements on the western frontier in those days. The school periodically served as a church on Sundays. Before leaving Kentucky for Illinois, Graham had taught in a first-rate building that survives today as a bed-and-breakfast in Greensburg. *Author's collection.*

had read on theology. "He took the passage, 'As in Adam all die, so in Christ shall all be made alive,' and followed with the proposition that whatever the breach or injury of Adam's transgression, which no doubt was great, was made just and right by the atonement of Christ."[186]

A week later, Lincoln asked Graham for the manuscript and took it to the store of Sam Hill. Parthena Hill recalled that Lincoln "wrote something on the subject of religion, which he intended for a pamphlet, and he brought it into the store, which was a great gathering place, and read it out to the crowd. Mr. Hill grabbed the pamphlet from him and said, 'Look here, Abe. The best thing you can do is to burn that and not tell anybody you ever wrote it.'"[187]

After his excommunication by the Hard-Shell Baptists over the issue of temperance, Graham openly criticized many of their practices, including foot washing. He tempted the wrath of Aunt Lizzy Greene, a "towel-woman," believing such rituals had nothing to do with being a good Christian.[188] Contrary to the Hard Shells, perhaps he shared Lincoln's viewpoint on hell and an Indian named Johnny Kongapod:

> *Here lies poor Johnny Kongapod.*
> *Have mercy on him, gracious God,*
> *As he would do if he was God*
> *And you were Johnny Kongapod.*[189]

While running for Congress in July 1846, Lincoln wrote a handbill in reply to a charge of his religious infidelity: "I am not a member of any Christian Church, is true, but I never denied the truth of the Scriptures; and I have never spoken with intentional disrespect of religion in general, or any denomination of Christians in particular." Then he went on to explain his philosophy: "It is true that in early life I was inclined to believe in what I understand is called the 'Doctrine of Necessity'…that the human mind is impelled to action, or held in rest by some power, over which the mind itself has no control." Lincoln closed his statement saying he had not argued the opinion for over five years. In addition, many Christian churches also held the same belief.[190]

II

Sometime after his unsuccessful run for the state legislature, Lincoln had breakfast with the Graham family after staying overnight in their home. Mentor Graham later recalled their conversation:

> *Mr. Lincoln spoke to me…and said, "I had a notion of studying grammar." I replied to him…"If you ever expect to go before the public in any capacity, I think it the best thing you can do." He said to me, "If I had a grammar I would commence now." There was none in the village and I said to him—"I know of a grammar at one Vance's about 6 miles [away]"…[Lincoln] got up and went on foot to Vance's and got the book. He soon came back and told me he had it. He then turned*

*his immediate and almost undivided attention to English grammar. The
book was* Kirkham's Grammar...*It was here that he commenced the
English grammar with me.*[191]

Lincoln also sought the help of others while studying Samuel Kirkham's
book, a difficult and complicated presentation. The author divided
grammar into four parts: orthography, etymology, syntax and prosody.
The student had to learn by rote memorization. To check on progress,
review questions were found at the end of each section. Graham's cousins
also played a role in Lincoln's pursuit of proper grammar. Bill Greene
asked Lincoln the review questions, and years later, Lincoln jokingly
introduced him to the cabinet as his teacher of grammar.[192] McNulty
Greene remembered Lincoln "studying it [Kirkham's book] on the hill
sides of old Salem. I spent several days giving him instruction in this
manner. In fact all the instruction he ever had in Grammar he rec'd from
me."[193] Either McNulty Greene did not know of the help his cousin and
brother had given to Lincoln or he wanted to take all of the credit for
himself. Lincoln later gave the book to a sister of Ann Rutledge.[194]

Taking time out from his studies, Lincoln earned his keep by doing odd
jobs around New Salem. On January 23, 1833, Lincoln tried to repair
a bed in James Rutledge's tavern. He needed a tool and sent Rutledge's
daughter, Nancy, to Row Herndon's cabin. "Mr. Herndon was loading his
gun to go hunting, and in getting ready to go out his gun was accidentally
discharged, and his wife, who was sitting near, talking to me, was shot
through the neck. I saw blood spurt out of each side of her neck, her
hands flutter for a moment." In terror, not only from the death of her
teacher's sister but also of her own close call, Nancy "flew out of the
house and hurried home and told Annie [her sister] and Lincoln." Years
later, she said, "I can never forget how sad and shocked they looked, after
having been so merry over their work just a moment before."[195]

Lincoln may have written the article that appeared two days later in
the *Sangamo Journal*:

*We learn that on Wednesday last, while Mr. R. Herndon of New
Salem was preparing his rifle for a hunting excursion, it went off, and*

On the original road into New Salem, the stagecoach first passed Clary's store and Offutt's store and then John Rowan Herndon's residence before stopping at the New Salem Tavern. Herndon married Mentor Graham's sister before leaving Green County, Kentucky, in 1830. A sign on the reconstructed cabin tells of the tragedy that occurred on this site: "On January 18, 1833, Rowan accidentally shot and killed his wife Elizabeth. Soon afterward he moved to Island Grove Township in Sangamon County." *Author's collection.*

the ball, striking his wife in the neck, separated one of the principal arteries, and in a few moments she was a corpse—It is hardly possible to conceive the anguish of the husband on this melancholy catastrophe. The community in which he lives deeply sympathizes with him in this afflicting event.[196]

Thomas Onstot remembered the gossip around New Salem that Row Herndon "acquired notoriety by shooting and killing his wife. Whether accidental or on purpose the people were about equally divided in their opinions. He was fooling with a loaded gun and it went off and killed her."[197] The rumors angered Herndon, who moved to Island Grove, where he remarried. Later that same year, the Grahams had a daughter, whom they named Elizabeth Herndon Graham. Row Herndon never mentioned the tragic incident in an 1865 letter to

William H. Herndon: "[T]he fall or winter of 32 or 33, I sold him [Lincoln] my stock of goods…on credit and some time after I cannot recollect as I left there for a while."[198]

III

Within a year, Lincoln had sold his interest in the store, and the homeless debtor moved in with the Grahams. During his six-month stay, Lincoln earned his room and board by doing chores around the farm, but Mentor

In the autumn of 1831, the Herndon brothers built a store in New Salem. James Herndon sold his share to William Berry in the summer of 1832. Later in the year, Lincoln bought Rowan Herndon's interest in the store. The following January, they moved to a larger location across the street. The replica of the first Berry-Lincoln Store was built in the 1930s, like most of the structures at New Salem Historic Site. In 1940, the U.S. postmaster general opened a post office in the store. *Author's collection.*

Graham owed him a debt of gratitude from the previous autumn: "I was unable for several weeks to do any work, and we were without means and in much distress. I was walking pass Lincoln's boarding-house one day when he came out and asked me about the family. I told him my little girl was dead. (And sister Nancy Ellen lay critically ill.) He appeared much affected."[199] Graham carried a small sack of corn, which needed to be ground into meal at the mill. Sarah Graham planned to bake corn bread, the solitary fare for supper that night. He desperately needed money for food and medicine for Nancy Ellen to regain her health.[200] "When I came back he handed me ten dollars, probably all the money he had in the world. I had not asked him for any and did not suppose he knew I needed it."[201]

In the meantime, women in the neighborhood complained about Sam Hill, the postmaster, who made them wait for their letters while he served whiskey to his customers. They successfully circulated a petition to remove Hill. Lincoln became postmaster on May 7, 1833, serving for three years until the post office moved to Petersburg. His income, no more than thirty dollars annually, came from a percentage of the postage paid by the receiver of the mail. The stagecoach delivered the mail on Thursdays and Saturdays. Lincoln worked only a few days each week at the back of Hill's store.[202] Since President Jackson appointed him, Lincoln claimed "the office [was] too insignificant, to make his politics an objective."[203] He made pocket money and read newspapers that arrived for subscribers.

While postmaster, Lincoln told Sam Hill a story about Johnson Elmore, a cousin of Mentor Graham. Many years later, James Miles gave his version of the story to William H. Herndon:

> [A]n ignorant, but ostentatious—proud man, used to go to Lincoln P.O. Every day—sometimes 3 or 4 times a day—if in town, and inquire—"Anything for me"—This bored Lincoln—yet it amused him: L. fixed a plan—wrote a letter to Johnson as coming from a negress in Ky.—saying many good things about opposum,—dances—corn shuckings—&c. and ending—"Johns—Come & see me and old master won't kick you out of the kitchen anymore"—[He] pretended to read

it—went & got some friends to read it—read it correctly—thought the reader was fooling him—went to others—with the same results—At last Johnson said he would get Lincoln to read it—presented it to L: it was almost too much for him—read it. The man never asked afterwards—"Anything here for me."[204]

A more lucrative job offer came to Lincoln in autumn: deputy surveyor for Sangamon County. "He accepted, procured a compass and chain, studied Flint, and Gibson a little, and went at it. This procured bread, and kept soul and body together."[205] Still living with the Grahams, Lincoln asked the schoolteacher for help. Mentor Graham had done some surveying in Kentucky after being taught by Nathaniel Owens at Brush Creek Academy. Owens had been a deputy surveyor who established the border in 1792 between the counties of Green and Hardin. Mentor Graham's grandfather helped Owens, his son-in-law.[206] Although only a child in the summer of 1835, Elizabeth Bell later heard the often-told story of her father and Lincoln:

Mr Lincoln knew nothing much originally about surveying. After he had surveyed a piece of land—getting corners—distances—directions &c he would call at our house…My father & Lincoln would sit till midnight calculating, unless mother would drive them out to get wood for cooking or for Sunday. Lincoln would say to mother—"Its too hard Mrs. Graham to disturb you so—but never mind, Mentor and myself will go out and get you wood." Father would hitch up the oxen and father and Lincoln would go out and soon return with great tree tops… rails having been made out of the stump end or first cut. When the wood was got in and cut up then Lincoln & father would sit up till midnight or later calculating the figures.[207]

Elizabeth Bell also recalled a humorous tale from those early times: "Mother went away one day to see friends who had just come from Kentucky leaving Lincoln and a large girl Polly, who was ugly and awkward, to keep house while she was gone." They decided to do some cooking and "broke so many dishes and spoiled so much food."

Then Lincoln tried to make "a hoe cake and put a handful of salaratus instead of salt in it." When Lincoln saw Sarah Graham approaching the house, he "ran down the road in the mud without a hat to announce his bad luck."[208]

At another time, Lincoln offered Elizabeth's brother, Simpson Graham, a jackknife "if he would kiss a certain pretty girl as she went to school… Simp met the girl—stepped up [and] put both hands on her cheeks and made the attempt to kiss her—but the girl was equal to the occasion." Carrying a jug of milk to have with her lunch, "the girl broke [it] on Simpson's head, the milk bespattering his jeans clothes." Lincoln had a good laugh and gave him the knife anyway "for his attempt."[209]

Three years later, Mentor Graham and Thomas J. Nance sat in Caleb Carman's house and recorded votes for the presidential election of 1836. Unable to agree on a candidate to oppose Martin Van Buren, the Whigs ran three candidates with strong regional support: Daniel Webster (Massachusetts), Hugh L. White (Tennessee) and William Henry Harrison (Ohio). They hoped to deny the Democrats an electoral majority, and the House of Representatives would then select a Whig for president. Only the names of Van Buren and White appeared on the ballot in Illinois. Many in New Salem precinct, including Bennett Abell, decided not to vote for any of the nominees. Mentor Graham and Bowling Green voted for White.[210]

After voting for Van Buren, McNulty Greene greeted his cousins Elizabeth Abell and Mary Owens, who had just gotten out of the stagecoach from Havana, Illinois. "None of the Poets or Romance writers have ever given to us a picture of a heroine so beautiful as a good description of Miss Owens in 1836…[She had] fair skin, deep blue eyes, with dark curling hair."[211]

Graham also saw them passing through town. Polly, as he called Mary Owens, was "good natured [with an] excellent disposition…She was a very intellectual person, well educated and well raised…free and social [with] beautiful and even teeth. [Even though] gay and lively [with] mirthfulness [which was] predominant [she had a] bilious temperament…Her mind was better cultivated than Miss Rutledge…She dressed neatly—gaudily never, though she could well have afforded it."[212]

Later in the day, Lincoln voted for Hugh H. White, who won the precinct but lost Illinois and the presidency to Van Buren. "[U]pon hearing of her [Mary Owens's] arrival in the neighborhood," Lincoln walked out of Carman's house thinking about Elizabeth Abell's matchmaking. "[I]t appeared to me, that her coming so readily showed that she was a trifle too willing; but…she might have been prevailed on by her married sister to come, without anything concerning me ever having been mentioned to her."[213]

6

OWENS
Fare Thee Well

I

In November 1836, Lincoln saw Mary Owens at the Abell homestead
for the first time in three years. She appeared different from what he
remembered. Maybe Lincoln had already gotten cold feet, like the time
he put off marrying Mary Todd. He might also have been worried
about his health. In January 1891, William H. Herndon wrote a letter
to Jesse Weik:

> *About the year 1835–1836, Mr. Lincoln went to Beardstown and
> during a devilish passion had connection with a girl and caught the
> disease* [syphilis]. *Lincoln told me this…About the year 1836–1837,
> Lincoln moved to Springfield…I supposed the disease hung to him and
> not wishing to trust our physicians, wrote a letter to Doctor Drake…
> Lincoln was a man of terribly strong passions but was true as steel to
> his wife during his whole marriage life; his honor, as Judge Davis has
> said, saved many a woman, and is most emphatically true as I know.*[214]

In spite of his anxieties, Lincoln courted her, and once again they
shared the joy of reading poetry together. "Lincoln had grown very fond
of Mary Owens," Bill Greene recalled, "and she seemed to take a fancy
to him. They were together a good deal, and finally, as was understood,

became engaged."[215] The courtship, however, did not go smoothly. One afternoon, they were visiting the Bowling Greens when she decided to go back up the hill to the Abell cabin. Nancy Green joined her. In an 1881 newspaper article, Bill Greene gave his account of the story:

> *Lincoln went with them. As usual Nancy took the baby* [Bowling Green Jr.] *and trudged along with it, although it was a heavy weight for her. Perhaps she expected that Lincoln would offer to shoulder the boy himself for part of the distance, and relieve her, but…he put his hands in his pockets and leisurely sauntered by the side of Mary Owens, without a glance toward the baby. Pretty soon Mary became cold, and answered Lincoln with short and curt sentences. Then she refused to talk to him at all, and by the end of the journey was reached she fairly withered him with her glances.*[216]

Johnson Greene visited his cousin in Weston, Missouri, in 1866. Mary (Owens) Vineyard told him her version of the story, which he related to William H. Herndon: "Lincoln did not appear to notice the old lady's struggles and when they got up to the house—say 100 ft and pretty steep, Miss Owens said to Lincoln—laughingly—'You would not make a good husband Abe.' [T]hey sat on the fence and one word brought on another, till a split or breach ensued."[217]

For the next couple of weeks, Lincoln attended the Tazewell County Circuit Court and then worked on his last surveys southwest of New Salem.[218] Upon his return, he saw Sam Abell in New Salem and inquired about his aunt. The boy told him she was at his parents' farm. Lincoln sent him home with a message that he would "be down to see her in a few minutes." Sam gave the message to Mary Owens, who had made plans to visit the Graham family. At the same time, she wanted to see if Lincoln was truly sorry for their quarrel and "thought a moment and said to herself, if I can draw Lincoln up there to the Grahams it will all be right."[219]

Elizabeth Abell met Lincoln at the door and told him her sister had gone to see their cousin, and he replied, "Didn't she know I was coming?" Trying to save her matchmaking, she told him, "No." But one

Sam Hill, a native of New Jersey, migrated to New Salem from Cincinnati, Ohio, in 1829. On July 28, 1835, he married Parthena Nance, a close friend of Mary Owens. They lived in the finest house in New Salem. Hill owned a store and a carding mill in the village. He was known as a shrewd businessman, thrifty and hot tempered. In 1918, a former resident of New Salem, Mrs. Louisa Clary, confirmed the sites of Hill's home and store, which were across the road from Dr. Allen's cabin. *Author's collection.*

of her children spoke out: "Yes, Ma—she did for I heard…Sam told her so." Lincoln came into the house and sat for a while, then decided to go back to the vacated post office in New Salem, where he still lived. Lincoln believed "that as he was extremely poor and Miss Owens very rich that it was a fling on him on that account. This was at that time Abe's tender spot."[220]

Shortly before attending the December session of the legislature in Vandalia, Lincoln met with Mary Owens, a get-together that may have been arranged by Elizabeth Abell. The weather continued to be unusually warm for late autumn, perhaps seen by them as a good sign of things to come. Since letters were soon exchanged, they apparently agreed to write to each other. Perhaps being apart was best for them at this stage of their relationship. They would have time to think about the prospect of marriage.[221]

In Vandalia, Lincoln felt sick and depressed, and he wrote to Mary Owens on December 13: "I have very little even yet to write. And the longer I can avoid the mortification of looking in the Post Office for your letter and not finding it, the better." Lincoln may have been thinking about her criticism of his manners when he said, "You see I am mad about that old letter yet. I don't like very well to risk you again. I'll try you once more any how."[222] Then he changed the subject to legislative news, which included John Taylor's petition for the new county of Menard and the attempt to move the state capital from Vandalia to Springfield. In conclusion, he wrote:

> *I believe I am about well now; but that, with other things I can not account for, have conspired and have gotten my spirits so low, that I feel that I would rather be any place in the world than here. I really can not endure the thought of staying here ten weeks. Write back soon as you get this, and if possible say something that will please me, for really I have not been pleased since I left you. This letter is so dry and stupid that I am ashamed to send it, but with my present feelings I can not do any better. Give my respects to Mr. and Mrs. Abell and family.*[223]

Lincoln later recalled those gloomy days with a different twist to the story: "I had letters from her, which did not change my opinion of either her intellect or intention; but on the contrary, confirmed it in both." But he had been having serious doubts about accepting her sister's matchmaking: "I found I was continually repenting the rashness, which had led me to make it. Through life I have been in no bondage, either real or imaginary from the thralldom of which I so much desire to be free." Elizabeth Abell, however, was "a great friend of mine." And he had promised to marry her sister "for better or for worse; and I made a point of honor and conscience in all things, to stick to my word." Even though Lincoln appeared to like a plump woman (i.e., Mary Todd), he began to exaggerate in his mind that she was overweight. "Exclusive of this, no woman that I have seen, has a finer face."[224]

Three days after Lincoln's letter to Mary Owens, a winter storm blew in from the prairie. First came a heavy, cold rain in the morning, and then the temperature dropped suddenly during the afternoon as the wind swept in from the northwest. Ponds and streams quickly froze. Chickens and geese were caught fast in the congealed mud. The bitter cold left Illinoisans with frost bite, and some were later found frozen to death. Like the winter of 1830–31, "The Sudden Change," as it was called, would become another benchmark in the lives of those who looked back to pioneer days in Illinois.[225]

Mary Owens spent the last day of the year with the Abells huddled before their blazing fireplace. The sisters probably remembered other New Year's Eves back in Kentucky when their mother was still alive. Her Scotch-Irish heritage came out in her manner of speaking. A certain song was already becoming a tradition at this time of the year. Although credited to Robert Burns, it had been sung in Scotland with varying lyrics since the early eighteenth century:

For auld lang syne, my dear,
For auld lang syne,
We'll take a cup o' kindness yet
For auld lang syne!

Should auld acquaintance be forgot,
And never brought to mind?
Should auld acquaintance be forgot,
And auld lang syne!

II

A month later, Illinoisans welcomed an early winter thaw after the frigid weather that had caused a terrible loss of livestock. On a Friday evening in February, Mary Owens most likely attended a meeting of the newly formed Rock Creek Lyceum to hear Thomas J. Nance debate a topic of interest to her: "Which is the greatest of the two evils, Slavery or Intemperance in the United States?"[226] Any romantic feelings on her part had presumably ended with Nance's marriage. Some two years earlier, she had written to him, "You will not fail to present my love to your Father & Mother in a particular manner, not forgetting Allen and Parthena, and except for yourself, the sincere regard of your friend."[227]

The lyceum met in a schoolhouse about four miles from the Abell farm. Bill Greene often served on juries that determined which side won the debate. According to the minutes of February 17, 1837, "A number of spectators…The side of slavery gained [won]. Affirmative, Messrs. Bagy, Bone, Black, and others; Negative, Messrs. Mr. President, Nance, Wynn and others. The house then chose for future discussion: 'The reduction of the price of the Public Lands.' A motion for adjournment carried."[228]

In early March, another topic might have been of interest to her: "Which is the greatest of all evils?" Seven members each took an evil to embrace: laziness, lying, ignorance, pride, slavery, neglect of duty and immoderate love of gain. One of James Goldsby's sons took the position

Dr. John Allen graduated from Dartmouth Medical School in 1828. In the summer of 1831, he came to New Salem and built a cabin to be used as a residence and doctor's office. Allen started the first Temperance Society, which met in his home. Nevertheless, patients often paid him with bushels of ground corn, which he had distilled and shipped to St. Louis. Mary Owens became a member of the temperance movement in Kentucky and may have attended meetings in New Salem while living with the Abells. *Author's collection.*

of slavery. (The Goldsbys were major slave owners back in Green County, Kentucky.) A three-man jury believed Lewis B. Wynn, a blacksmith and secretary of the club, argued the best case for ignorance. Later in the month, Mary Owens would have been pleased when a jury decided intemperance was "the greatest of all evils since the fall of Adam."[229]

Making reference to her father, who operated a still, and an uncle, who could not stay sober, Mary Owens had written Nance the previous year:

> *I can with pleasure say to you that the infant cause of Temperance which you left has almost grown to manhood, shedding abroad its benign influence through the land. We now and then have an opposer on the subject but they are fast hiding their diminishing heads before the bursts of light perceptible to the most casual observer. From Mr. Henry, I learned the opposition you met with among your anti-Temperance friends and some of them I fear are allied to me by ties of consanguinity.*[230]

Besides founding the first Sunday school in New Salem, Dr. John Allen also organized the first temperance society, the White Templars or Washingtonians. Thomas J. Nance spoke on the subject to his fellow members. "I presume that temperance, in the acceptance of the term, has been much the theme of ridicule if not misrepresentation. From the change required by this reformation in the use of ardent spirits, I have always expected opposition…We have united hoping to dry up some of the deepest fountains of disease, crime, poverty, blasphemy, indolence, needless taxes, orphans' tears, and widows' broken hearts."[231] In spite of supporting temperance, Dr. Allen usually distilled his "pay-corn," a fee he charged his patients. He shipped the whiskey to St. Louis. In a region of poor transportation, farmers found it more profitable to send their excess harvests to market as four barrels of liquor rather than twenty-four bushels of corn.

Distillers also supplied a local demand for whiskey. George Warburton, a merchant and co-founder of Petersburg, drowned in the Sangamon River after a drunken spree. Peter Lunkins met the same fate, and Lincoln's business partner, William Berry, ruined his health by excessive drinking. Liquor saw wide use as a medicine and at social gatherings, including funerals, weddings, birthdays, holidays and election campaigns. Not to serve whiskey was considered inhospitable. Overindulgence often led to fights and other abusive behavior.

Jeremiah Graham, Mary Owens's uncle, had been expelled because of drunkenness from the New Salem Baptist Church. Mentor Graham, his son, used the church on Greene's Rocky Branch as his schoolhouse. When Mentor Graham joined the White Templars, church members also expelled him because the predestinarian congregation believed temperance societies were contrary to matters that were predestined by God. A church member reportedly asked, "Now, brethering, how much of this critter [jug of whiskey] have I got to drink to have good standing amongst you?"[232]

Lincoln's conversations with Mary Owens about temperance most likely included some of his thoughts in 1842. In an address before the Washington Temperance Society of Springfield, he alluded to reformers like Mary Owens, who "are practical philanthropists...Benevolence and charity possess their hearts entirely...And when such is the temper of the advocate, and such the audience, no good cause can be unsuccessful." However, he may not have told her that "it is not much in the nature of man to be driven to anything, still less to be driven about that which is exclusively his own business." Near the end of the address, he touched on another hope for the future that she at one time shared with him: "And when the victory shall be complete—when there shall be neither a slave nor a drunkard on the earth— how proud the title of that Land, which... shall have planted, and nurtured to maturity, both the political and moral freedom of their species."[233]

In those days, a kind of slavery did exist in Illinois. Richard E. Bennett, a neighbor of the Abells, had a servant whose parents had signed her over to him:

This Indenture of Apprentice made and entered into this 26th day of September 1836: Witnesseth that Sarah Miller a mulatto girl aged ten years on the 1st day of January 1836, of her own free will—consent and agreement and by and with the consent and agreement of Isabella Thorton her mother and of Charles Thornton her stepfather hereto affixed and by and with the approbation of Boling Green [sic] *and John Clary two acting Justices of the Peace in and for Sangamon County hath put placed and bound herself to Richard E. Bennett…until she…shall attain the age of eighteen years.*[234]

Free or otherwise, Afro-Americans were not popular in Illinois. In a lead article on November 7, 1835, the *Sangamon Journal* announced, "Our State is threatened to be overrun with free negroes."[235] At the time, the population of the county, yet to be divided, was eighteen thousand, of whom seventy-eight were free blacks, six slaves and twenty registered black indentured servants.[236] Nearly a year and a half later, Lincoln and Dan Stone, another representative from Sangamon County, presented a protest before the state legislature over a resolution passed in January. "They believe that the institution of slavery is founded on both injustice and bad policy; but that the promulgation of Abolitionist doctrines tends rather to increase than abate its evils." They went on to declare that Congress could not legally interfere with slavery within the states, but under the Constitution, had the power to abolish it in the District of Columbia.[237]

III

On March 7, 1837, Lincoln rode out of Vandalia with William Butler of Springfield. They stayed over night in Henderson's Point. A depressed Lincoln told him, "I am going home, Butler, without a thing in the world. I have drawn all my pay I got at Vandalia, and have spent it all. I am in debt—I am owing Van Bergan, and he has levied on my horse and my compass…I don't know what to do."[238] The debt dated back to 1833, when John Vineyard and Albert Williams foreclosed on Reuban Radford. Later, Van Bergan purchased the note and sued Lincoln, getting a judgment on his horse.

When they arrived in Springfield, Butler sold Lincoln's horse without telling him and then paid off the debt to Van Bergan using some of his own money. Upon finding out, Lincoln was "greatly astonished," although he did not know until a year later that the entire debt had been paid. "He said he had to go down home to New Salem. I told him that he might take my horse and ride him down there. I also told him there were his saddlebags, [Butler's wife had washed Lincoln's clothes] and that there was a clean shirt in them. He took the saddlebags and went and got the horse, and rode down to New Salem."[239]

Lincoln may not have disclosed to the Abells or Mary Owens why he was riding a different horse. Since their brothers-in-law had sold the note that Radford originally held on Lincoln and Berry, he probably refrained from embarrassing them and himself. The talk around the Abell household concerned a move to another county. Northern Sangamon County seemed more every year like a backwater region with no future. Now with a panic hitting the economy, things would only get worse. The Abells were serious enough with their plans that Lincoln mentioned his feelings in a letter to Mary Owens: "Tell your sister I don't want to hear anymore about selling out and moving. That gives me the hypo [depression] whenever I think of it."[240]

A month later, Lincoln moved to Springfield and called less frequently on the Abells. Their cabin seemed to always have the scent of meals past and present. Elizabeth Abell cooked many of them in her Dutch oven hanging over the flames in the fireplace. Chicken and soft dumplings were a particular favorite around New Salem, in addition to pancakes, flapjacks and corn cakes fried on an iron skillet sitting on a bed of hot embers.[241] Lincoln often said, "[H]e could eat corn cakes as fast as two women could make them."[242]

IV

In early spring, Lincoln and Mary Owens rode their horses down the trail from the Abell farm and followed the road into New Salem. They came into the sleepy town, passing some of the now-vacant cabins. Within a few years, Sam Hill's store, the last one in New Salem, would be moved to Petersburg. Taking the road to the left, they rode by the cabin built by Isaac Gulihur, who had left for Knox County, Illinois. Even though the streams were high and the trails muddy, they were joined by other couples along the way. The party left the town behind them and approached Greene's Rocky Branch, beyond which was the cemetery and, farther along, the Baptist church where Mentor Graham taught school. Writing to William H. Herndon in 1866, Mary (Owens) Vineyard recalled that long-ago day:

> *There was a company of us going to Uncle Billy Greens, Mr. L. was riding with me, and we had a very bad branch to cross, the other gentlemen were very officious in seeing that their partners got over safely; we were behind, he riding in never looking back to see how I got along; when I rode up beside him, I remarked, you are a nice fellow; I suppose you did not care whether my neck was broken or not. He laughingly replied, (I suppose by way of compliment) that he knew I was plenty smart to take care of myself.*[243]

She knew Lincoln's sensitivity to animals and may have reasoned that a hog was to be treated like a lady by him and a lady like a hog:

> *He told me of an incident; that he was crossing a prairie one day, and saw before him a hog mired down, to use his own language; he was rather fixed up (dressed up) and he resolved that he would pass on without looking toward the shoat, after he had gone by, he said the feeling was eresistable [sic] and he had to look back, and the poor thing seemed to say so wistfully—There now! my last hope is gone; that he deliberately got down and he relieved it from difficulty.*[244]

Soon afterward, Lincoln's conduct again upset her. Elizabeth Abell had been entertaining friends and suggested they take a walk to pick wild flowers. She carried her baby son, William. A niece later described the outing: "Before entering this pasture there was a little streamlet to cross, with stepping stones, some close together others far apart, which made it difficult for a lady to cross. Mr. Lincoln went first, the others crossed as best they could. Aunt Pop [Mary was also called Polly or Pop] was so dismayed that he did not carry the baby."[245] Irene Buckles, another niece, looked back on what she had heard from her mother, Lizzie Babbitt (née Abell):

Aunt Mary was reared in Southern aristocracy with servants to wait upon her and all deference shown her—gallant gentlemen eager to assist her at all times. It is not surprising to me that she did not fall in love with Mr. Lincoln. I like to think that if she could have looked into the future and known that Mr. Lincoln would one day be President of this great United States, her answer would still have been "No." My grandmother, Mrs. Abell, seemed to have the premonition he would some day be famous and was anxious for her sister to marry him. But from the reports on Aunt Mary, I am sure she needed no one to help her find a husband. She was well educated, handsome, with a wonderful personality and even as she grew older, everyone loved her.[246]

At this stage of the courtship, Mary Owens might have felt trapped in a relationship bought on by her sister. At the same time, Lincoln's doubts of getting married, especially in his present state of poverty, began to

Anna Hyatt Huntington's equestrian statue of Lincoln stands on Route 97 close to the entrance of New Salem State Historic Site. *On the Circuit* casting duplicates can be seen in Lincoln City, Oregon; Syracuse, New York; and Salzburg, Austria. In 1837, while crossing a nearby creek on horses, Lincoln angered Mary Owens because he did not look back to see if she needed help. Laughing, he said she was smart enough to take care of herself. *Author's collection.*

trouble him again: "After my return, I saw nothing to change my opinion of her in any particular. She was the same and so was I. I now spent my time between planning how I might get along through life after my contemplated change of circumstances should have taken place; and how I might procrastinate the evil day for a time, which I really dreaded as much—perhaps more than an Irishman does the halter."[247]

For her part, Mary Owens saw the "qualities of the young man who was paying her such devoted attention. But while she admired, she did not love him. He was ungainly and angular in his physical make-up, and to her seemed deficient in the nicer and more delicate attentions, which she felt to be due from the man whom she had pictured as an ideal husband."[248]

Mary Owens often went to see Parthena Hill, who lived next door to her husband's store in New Salem. In warm weather, they sat on the porch and talked about old times back in Kentucky. In an earlier letter, she had playfully chided her: "Say to Parthena, if she is not married, that I will not ask a letter of her, but it would be gratefully received at any time, when she can from interest, or amusement, write to her neglected Friend."[249] Parthena later recalled her friend wanting to teach Lincoln a lesson because of his boast to marry her. "I don't think they ever became engaged, for Mary was a woman of too much character to go as far as that, and I don't think she ever got very much in earnest. She told me once that she didn't. But Mr. Lincoln thought a great deal of her, I expect."[250]

V

Lincoln now roomed with storekeeper Joshua F. Speed in Springfield. An advertisement in the *Sangamo Journal* announced to the public that "J.T. Stuart and A. Lincoln, Attorneys and Counselors at Law, will practice conjointly in the courts of this Judicial Circuit Office No. 4 Hoffman's Row upstairs."[251] In the meantime, Lincoln did not appear particularly pleased in a letter he wrote to Mary Owens in early May: "This thing of living in Springfield is a dull business after all, at least it is to me. I am quite as lonesome here as ever was anywhere in my life. I have been spoken to by but one woman since I've been here, and should not have been by her, if she could have avoided it. I've never been to church yet, nor probably shall not be soon. I stay away because I am conscious I should not know how to behave myself."[252]

The woman Lincoln referred to may have been Mary Todd, who was visiting her sister, Mrs. Ninian Edwards, in Springfield. A cousin of John T. Stuart, she very likely met his law partner, Lincoln, because of him.[253] Lincoln would have felt shy in the presence of the young belle from Lexington, Kentucky. He later courted her in the same indecisive way as he had Mary Owens. However, Mary Todd had deep feelings for him that Mary Owens did not share, and Lincoln, sensing this affinity, pursued the courtship even after jilting her the first time they were to be married.[254]

In the opening paragraph of his letter to Mary Owens, Lincoln admitted that he had difficulty in writing to her and had torn up two previous letters. He was trying to bring things out into the open but in his own indirect way:

I am often thinking about what we said of your coming to live in Springfield. I am afraid you would not be satisfied. [She probably wondered what he was trying to say.] *There is a great deal of flourishing about in carriages here, which it would be your doom to see without sharing in it. You would have to be poor without the means of hiding your poverty.* [She may have told him about her father's tightness with money.] *Whatever woman may cast her lot with mine, should any ever do, it is my intention to do all in my power to make her happy and contented; and there is nothing I can imagine, that would make me more unhappy than to fail in the effort. I know I should be much happier with you than the way I am, provided I saw no sign of discontent in you.*[255]

Mary Owens's remarks at Greene's Rocky Branch seemed to be fresh in his memory:

What you have said to me may have been in jest, or I may have misunderstood it. If so, then let it be forgotten; if otherwise, I much wish you think seriously before you decide. For my part I have already

Still preoccupied with his relationship with Mary Owens, Lincoln attended a banquet on August 3, 1837, in Athens, seven miles east of New Salem. Lincoln and eight other legislators had acquired the name of Long Nine because of their height. On the second floor of Mathew Roger's general store, they were honored for supporting the move of the state capital from Vandalia to Springfield. Two years later, a resident of Athens complained to Lincoln about the town now being in the new county of Menard. *Author's collection.*

decided. What I have said I will most positively abide by, provided you wish it. My opinion is that you had better not do it. You have not been accustomed to hardship, and it may be more severe than you can imagine. I know you are capable of thinking correctly on any subject; and if you deliberated maturely upon this, before you decide, then I am willing to abide your decision. You must write me a good long letter after you get this.[256]

On the morning of August 16, Lincoln rode up the bluff to the Abell cabin. However, the meeting did not resolve the matter, and he returned to Springfield. Lincoln wrote to Mary Owens that evening, probably repeating his words from earlier in the day:

You must know that I can not see you, or think of you, with entire indifference; and yet it may be, that you, are mistaken in regards to what my real feelings towards you are. I want in all cases to do right, and most particularly so, in all cases with women. I want, at this particular time, more than any thing else, to do right with you, and if I knew it would be doing right, as I suspect it would, to let you alone, I would do it…If you feel yourself in any degree bound to me, I am willing to release you, provided you wish it; while on the other hand, I am willing, and even anxious to bind you faster, if I can be convinced that it will, in any considerable degree, add to your happiness. This, indeed, is the whole question with me. Nothing would make me more miserable than to believe you miserable—nothing more happy, than to know you were so…

You will, no doubt, think it rather strange, that I should write you a letter on the same day on which we parted; and I can only account for it by supposing, that seeing you lately makes me think of you more than usual, while at our late meeting we had few expressions of thoughts…And for the purpose of making the matter as plain as possible, I now say, that you can now drop the subject, dismiss your thoughts (if you ever had any) from me forever, and leave this letter unanswered, without calling me forth one accusing murmur from me. And I will even go further, and say, that if it will add any thing to your comfort, or peace of mind, to do so, it is my sincere wish that you should. Do not understand by this, that I wish to cut your acquaintance. I mean no such thing.[257]

Appearing incapable of resolving the dilemma himself, Lincoln pressured Mary Owens to make the final decision. "What I do wish is, that our further acquaintance shall depend upon yourself. If such further acquaintance would contribute nothing to your happiness, I am sure it would not to mine…If it suits you best to not answer this— farewell—a long life and a merry one attend you. But if you conclude to write back, speak as plainly as I do. There can be neither harm nor danger, in saying, to me, any thing you think, just in the manner you think it." He closed with "respects to your sister" and may have been thinking that Elizabeth Abell was the one who had gotten them into this predicament.[258]

Mary Owens felt that even though her sister "was very anxious for us to be married, that I thought Mr. Lincoln was deficient in those little links which make up the great chain of woman's happiness, at least it was so in my case; not that I believed it proceeded from a lack of goodness of heart, but his training had been different from mine, hence there was not that congeniality which would have otherwise existed." In the end, she made the decision for the both of them. "[H]is heart and hand were at my disposal, and I suppose my feelings were not sufficiently enlisted to have the matter consummated."[259]

On April 1, 1838, Lincoln described their last meeting in a letter to Mrs. Orville H. Browning, wife of a colleague in the legislature:

> *I mustered my resolution, and made the proposal to her direct: but shocking to relate, she answered, No. At first I supposed she did it through an affectation of modesty…but on my renewal of the charge, I found she repelled it with greater firmness than before. I tried again and again, but with the same success, or rather with the same want of success. I finally was forced to give it up…I was mortified, it seemed to me, in a hundred different ways…I had so long been too stupid to discover her intentions, and at the same time never doubting that I understood them perfectly.*[260]

Lincoln gave an absurd impression of Mary Owens, which might have been an expression of his resentment toward her:

> *I knew she was over-sized, but she now appeared a match for Falstaff. I knew she was called an "old maid"…but now when I beheld her, I could not for my life avoid thinking of my mother; and this without withered features, for her skin was too full of fat, to permit its contracting in to wrinkles; but from her want of teeth, weathered-beaten appearance in general…nothing could have commenced at the size of infancy, and reached her present bulk in less than thirty five or forty years; and in short, I was not at all pleased with her. But what could I do? I had told*

*her sister that I would take her for better or for worse; and I made a point
of honor and conscience to stick to my word.*[261]

Perhaps Lincoln's letter to a friend was only an April Fools Day tale to
amuse her. (While president, he told Mrs. Orville H. Browning to keep
the letter private because it was based on an actual incident in his life.)[262]
The letter closed with a pledge that he would "never again think of
marrying; and for this reason; I can never be satisfied with any one who
would be block-head enough to have me."[263]

Benjamin R. Vineyard believed his mother "acted honorably with Mr.
Lincoln…[and] took no unladylike course, to reject the offered hand of
Mr. Lincoln."[264]

"His honesty of purpose showed itself in all his efforts to win her hand.
He told her of his poverty and while advising her that life with him meant
to her, who had been reared in comfort and plenty, great privation and
sacrifice, yet he wished to secure her as a wife. But she felt she did not
entertain for him the same feeling that he professed for her." Early in their
relationship, she had heard rumors "of his determination to marry her,
and not being certain of the sincerity of his purposes, may have purposely
left him…somewhat in uncertainty. But later on, when, by his manner and
his repeated announcement to her that his hand and heart were at her
disposal, she declined his offer kindly but with no uncertain meaning."[265]

Being fond of poetry, Mary Owens and Lincoln knew a particular
verse by Lord Byron that may have come to mind when they parted in
the late summer of 1837: "Fare thee well! And if forever, / Still forever,
fare thee well."

VI

Mary Owens stayed on with the Abells another eight months. She left
for Kentucky a week or so after her sister gave birth to a daughter,
Serepta, on April 8, 1838. During those months, one wonders if she had
overstayed her welcome. Accustomed to being attended by slaves, she
had to help around the cabin so as not to be a burden to her sister. While

The interior of Bennett and Elizabeth Abell's home might have been comparable to Dr. Francis Regnier's cabin. During her second stay with the Abell family, Mary Owens spent over a year with them. She obviously felt at home after leaving her father's splendid house in Kentucky. Moreover, there were no slaves to wait on her. Assumingly, she helped her sister with the children, housework and cooking. The Abells owned a ladder-back chair made in Kentucky, similar to the one on the right side of the picture. Lea Thomas inherited the chair from her mother. *Author's collection.*

Bennet Abell worked in the fields, Elizabeth Abell typically "looked after the larder, planning meals, pickling, preserving fruit and vegetables, smoking and storing meats and game…making soap…along with the other chores and duties of the frontier housewife and mother."[266] Perhaps Mary Owens did not go back to Kentucky right after the breakup with Lincoln because it might have looked like she had originally come only to find a husband. Once the cold rain and snow of late autumn and early winter set in, it was easier to wait for spring.

In April 1838, Mary Owens said goodbyes to her relatives and left for Kentucky. Her relationship with Lincoln had ended, but she remained an influence in his search for a wife. Mary Todd had the same background as Mary Owens. Native-born Kentuckians, their fathers were wealthy slave owners. At six years of age, they lost their mothers and had problems adjusting to stepmothers. Highly educated females, they loved

English literature, especially poetry, and were splendid readers and good conversationalists who admired Henry Clay. Even Lincoln's courtship of them had similarities. Besides being reluctant to end his bachelorhood, he hesitated at marrying a woman accustomed to a higher standard of living than the one he might be able to provide.[267]

The following year, Mary Owens may have recommended Lincoln when her father needed an attorney to collect an old loan. Nathaniel Owens had assigned the note of John M. and George L. Cabiness to his son-in-law, Albert G. Williams. He sought payment of the debt, which dated back to 1822. The case was continued until the July 1839 session in the Springfield court. John M. Cabiness was now the only defendant, and Lincoln called Bennett Abell as a witness. The lawyer for Cabiness presented to the court "special matter in evidence of set-off to which plea the plaintiff filed his joiner." After a short deliberation, the eight jurors reached a verdict in favor of the defendant. The judge ruled, "It is therefore considered by the Court that the defendant recover of the plaintiff his costs by him about his defense therein expended."[268]

Besides the fee for Cabiness's lawyer, Albert G. Williams had to pay court costs. Bennett Abell did not get compensated for travel and food expenses until a year later. Williams was out nearly half the amount of the original loan, and Nathaniel Owens had to compensate him for his loses. Lincoln may not have gotten any fee because he lost the case.[269]

Elizabeth Abell brought a message from Lincoln when she visited Kentucky in 1840. A month before leaving Illinois, she had seen Lincoln in Springfield, and probably in jest he said, "Tell your sister Mary I think she was a great fool that she did not remain here and marry me." On hearing his comment, Mary Owens retorted, "Characteristic of the man."[270]

According to Nancy Vineyard, Mary Owens "had many offers of marriage from the best young men of her acquaintance, who, strange to say, always parted with her in friendship, and continued friendly towards her afterwards."[271] She was certainly a good match with her father's wealth, which would someday bring a nice inheritance. Perhaps she had been looking for too much in a husband and had little to choose from in provincial Green County, Kentucky. Nearing her thirty-third birthday, Mary Owens finally accepted a proposal of marriage, which may have come through the mail. Jesse Vineyard, her sister's brother-in-law, returned to Kentucky from Missouri, and the service took place in her father's home on March 17, 1841. Soon afterward, they departed for Weston Township in Platte County, Missouri.

Five of the six daughters of Nathaniel Owens now lived in Weston Township. Except for Elizabeth Abell, they had married men who became slave owners in Missouri. Jesse and Mary Vineyard's household in 1850 included their four children, a hired hand from Georgia and seven slaves.[272] Nearly four years earlier, heavy rains in the counties along the overflowing Missouri River had brought on an epidemic of typhoid fever. Tragedy struck the family, which Mary Vineyard recorded in the family Bible on January 21, 1847: "Nanny B. Vineyard first daughter of Jessie and Mary Vineyard born in Platte County, Mo. October 10, 1845 and died…age 15 months and 3 days."[273]

ABELL

A Very Life in Our Despair

I

Ever since the Panic of 1837, agricultural prices had slumped. It hardly paid to grow, harvest and transport crops to the towns on the Illinois River. By the middle of the 1850s, railroads connected the major cities of Illinois with Chicago as the hub of the growing network. The farmers of Menard County looked forward to the day when a railroad brought an affordable means of getting their crops to market. Even with the region's transportation and economic problems, the value of Bennett Abell's land increased dramatically.[274] He supplemented his income by doing work for the county, including road surveys and repairs. In addition, the Commissioners Court of Menard County paid Bennett Abell nineteen dollars for the three-month boarding of Nancy Armstrong, mother of Bowling Green and Jack Armstrong.[275]

On a cold Sunday evening in February 1842, Bowling Green climbed the path up the hill to the Abells' cabin. He had a huge belly and weighted over 250 pounds. Green had visited his neighbors on a regular basis, but this time the climb was unusually stressful. He walked into the Abell cabin, collapsed in a chair and died of a stroke. One of the Abell children ran to the Graham farm to share the bad news. Mentor and Sarah Graham joined the Abells in an effort to comfort Nancy Green. Since Bowling Green had been a good friend of Bennet Abell and Mentor

Bowling Green died on February 13, 1841, and was buried on the bluff near the Abell cabin. Sometime later, his remains were moved to Petersburg's Oakland Cemetery. In July 1862, Bowling Green Jr. joined the Eighty-fifth Illinois Volunteer Infantry. He served in Company E, the Menard County company. On July 19, 1864, Corporal Green suffered a severe wound at the Battle of Peach Tree Creek, Georgia, and died two months later in Kingston, Georgia. His gravestone is marked No. 471 in the Marietta National Cemetery. *Author's collection.*

Graham, more than likely they helped dig the grave in the frozen earth. On Tuesday, the weather was too cold for any formal funeral service as the widow and her nine children, along with friends and neighbors, gathered for the burial on the bluff north of Abell's cabin.[276]

Masonic services for Bowling Green were not held until September 1842. The Springfield Lodge No. 4 conducted memorial serves in Petersburg and at the grave site. John Bennett recalled that Nancy Green wanted Lincoln to give a eulogy. "When I delivered Mrs. Green's request to him, he remarked to me that he did not know what to say…I replied to him that it would gratify the old lady, if he would make some remarks on the occasion." Lincoln agreed and talked about Bowling Green's "manners, customs, habits of life." John Bennett thought Lincoln's eulogy was not very good, but "after all I don't know that it could be considered a failure, when we reflect that he had but little material to make a speech" and had been asked on the spur of the moment.[277]

According to one of his lawyer friends, Henry C. Whitney, Lincoln tried to give a funeral address and "ignominiously failed. His feelings overpowered him as the past rose in his fancy and the disinterested affection of his departed friend pasted in review; his sobs choked his utterance, and he withdrew from the mournful scene to accompany Mrs. Green to her desolate home."[278] During this stressful time, Lincoln may have recalled a line from his favorite poem by Lord Byron: "There is a very life in our despair."[279] Three days later, the Abells buried their two-year-old son, Gaines, near the grave of Bowling Green.

The following year, Bennett and Elizabeth Abell's son-in-law, McNulty Greene, was one of two defendants in a lawsuit. (Three years earlier, Greene had married his sixteen-year-old second cousin, Nancy O. Abell.) Lincoln and Stephen T. Logan represented the plaintive, William L. May, former leader of the Whigs in Springfield and now a ferry operator in Peoria. May contended that he owned a strip of land on the Illinois River that Greene and Joseph B. Loose claimed to be their property.[280]

In the Tazewell County Circuit Court, Lincoln and Logan charged that "on Sept. 24, 1838 one Lynn M. Green clerk in the Registers dept. Springfield together with Joseph B. Loose either for purposes of fraud or in ignorance, assumed the land…did not extend to the river…[Then] Green playing the part of Register made entry and purchased and altered plat." On behalf of their client, they asked that "such patient be declared null and void." They continued the case until the following year, when the defendants failed to appear, and the court ruled in favor of May.[281]

II

Raining almost every day, the summer of 1843 had been a terrible one for farming in Illinois. "I think the water…was six feet deep all over the land, and no crop was raised that year. A man could start at Coal Branch and go up through Goodpasture's land; then run through Bennett Able's [sic] farm, and land near Bowling Green's house. All the rails would be carried down and landed in the drifts across the river from Petersburg."[282] A few miles north of Petersburg, Charles Clark wrote a letter in July: "We have had some very heavy showers of rain, hail and wind which have done considerable damage in braking glass blowing down buildings and timber. The first of June there was a storm that blew down all our fences and laid our farms all common."[283]

In late autumn 1843, gossip filled the air over a trial about to take place in the Menard County courthouse. Eliza S. Cabot, a young teacher from New England, sued the eccentric doctor Francis Regnier for slander. She retained Lincoln and hoped to collect $5,000 in damages because Regnier had spread rumors about her and Elijah Taylor engaging in sexual intercourse. The alleged episode occurred in a Petersburg rooming house operated by Maria Bennett.[284] Although he later contributed to Lincoln's victory in the lawsuit, Bennett Abell did not join the curious spectators in the crowded courtroom. Trials were often akin to sporting events where the locals cheered for their favorites, like Lincoln.[285]

Sitting next to Miss Cabot, Lincoln took on the image of the protector of the forlorn teacher. Regnier pleaded not guilty, and then Judge Samuel Treat rejected the defendant's special plea of justification because he claimed his statement of Cabot's fornication was true. Elijah Taylor, John Bennett and Sam Hill, among a number of witnesses, testified that Regnier had made slanderous remarks about the plaintiff: "If people knew as much about her as I do they would think differently of her from what they do. [Thomas] Peak is honest in going to see her but Taylor is not. Taylor is after skin and he has got it…The Captain [Taylor] has got skin there as much as he wanted…You [Taylor] have ordered her and John Rogered [*sic*] her."[286]

The jury got the case and went to deliberate on the second floor of the courthouse. Instead of staying together, Hiram Stevens "saw several of said jurors leave the jury room, go down the stairs, without their fellow jurors, or any attending officer, and remain absent, for a considerable length of time." Later in the day, Calvin Pierce, jury foreman, read their decision: "We the jurors find a verdict in favor of the plaintiff of twelve dollars and cost."[287]

Lincoln wrote affidavits after talking to Hiram Stevens, Lewis Wynne and Bennet Abell.[288] Two days before the trial, Lewis Wynne had heard Pierce "say that he believed there would be but a very small verdict in said case, that he believed the plaintiff's character to be very bad." Bennett Abell swore that "before the trial of the same [suit] he at different times heard Calvin Pierce…say that he did not believe Miss Cabot ought to recover much if anything off F. Regnier for he did not believe she was the clean thing at any act, and that at other times his declarations on the subject were of like import."[289]

In his own affidavit, Calvin Pierce insisted that he had "no recollection of ever having any contact with Bennett Abel [*sic*] in relation to the case now pending in this Court…[and] saying any thing with Lewis Wynne or anybody against the Plaintiff or any thing injurious to the said Plaintiff Cabot." Going before Judge Samuel H. Treat, Lincoln, along with his law partners Edward D. Baker and Thomas L. Harris, motioned for a new trial because of five reasons: The jury's verdict was "contrary to the evidence." A member of the jury had formed "an opinion adverse to the plaintive." The jury had "improperly made up" its verdict. Members of the jury had shown "partiality" and "separated contrary to law." Judge Treat granted the motion, and another made by Lincoln, changing the venue of the case to Jacksonville in Morgan County.[290]

On March 15, 1844, a jury awarded damages of $1,600. Regnier, however, appealed the case to the Illinois Supreme Court, claiming that Judge Samuel D. Lockwood in the Circuit Court of Morgan County had made a mistake in refusing to allow certain evidence to prove the plaintiff's immoral character. In December 1845, the court upheld the verdict, believing Judge Lockwood had acted properly since he had given the defense the opportunity to prove Cabot's alleged bad character. Justice Norman H. Purple wrote that "character is too valuable to permit it, in a court of justice to be destroyed, or even sullied by a report derived from a majority of three persons only."[291]

Evidently, Regnier had no hard feelings toward Bennett Abell. Ill with cholera at the time, Oliver G. Abell suffered from dehydration caused by severe diarrhea. Regnier prescribed a "recipe for cholera: opium 2 grns, calomel 5 grs, sugar of lead 1½ grs, camphor 1¼, give every

Lizzie Abell was born in her parents' cabin south of Petersburg in 1841. During the Civil War, she went to Washington, where her brother, Oliver G. Abell, worked in the General Land Office. The Treasury Department employed her for about a year. After the war, she married John Babbitt, a Union army veteran, and they moved in 1870 to Atchison County, Missouri. Mary (Owens) Vineyard's son, Benjamin Vineyard, lived seventy-five miles south in St. Joseph. Whether she ever visited her cousin is unknown. Over the years, she enjoyed telling stories about her childhood memories of Lincoln. *Lea Thomas collection.*

½ hour till disease is arrested."[292] Cholera epidemics were common at a time when little was known about the origin of the disease and drinking water came from polluted wells. In spite of the treatment, the boy managed to survive. In 1861, President Lincoln appointed him to a government job in Washington.[293]

III

Elizabeth Abell received word that her father had died on June 1, 1844. A year earlier, Nathaniel Owens had been ill when he completed two poems.[294] "Ah when I lay in my sick bed / Righteous Jesus guard my head." Perhaps, he looked back to a lifetime spent owning and abusing slaves at Lashfield: "Now lord I hope my life to mend / Oh help me lord unto my end." In his other poem, Owens wrote of his wife thinking about her late husband:

My Jesus called my husband home
And here I'm lonely ever since
Relying when I'm called to come
Yea I will reach my heavenly home
Mighty Savior guide me on
Where all true penetants [sic] have gone

Ah may I stand at thy right hand
Rejoicing in that heavenly land
In company with my husband dear
Now I do hope to see him there
Great god for heaven all should prepare

A week before his death, Nathaniel Owen summoned his lawyer and a friend to witness his change of heart: "As my children grew up and married I gave them money bearing interest and hold their bonds for the same, but I now conclude it is best for me and best for them to pay no interest should any one or more of them have paid interest on their bonds it is to be deducted from the amount they have received from me."[295]

In 1872, William B. Allen wrote Nathaniel Owens's epitaph: "He was a farmer of good education of the times, and a high order of native intellect. He was a man of untiring perseverance and industry." During his lifetime, he became a very wealthy man who "was thought by many to be selfish in his disposition…He was a close, economical, money-making man, but punctiliously honest in all his dealings. He dispensed but little, if any, of his property to his children in his life-time, but they and their descendants received it all after his death."[296]

Bennett Abell went to Kentucky in August for the estate sale and to look after his wife's inheritance. He returned to Lashfield for the first time since leaving Kentucky almost fourteen years earlier to the day. Abell met his slave-owning brothers-in-law, with whom he had little in common. Besides the estate sale, Abell also had concerns about a loan for $238 that he had cosigned some years earlier when Felix G. Graham, his wife's cousin, and Jacob Victor borrowed the money from

Nathaniel Owens. (Debtors owed to the Owens estate nearly $17,000 plus interest.) Abell wanted to make sure the two of them would not default, leaving him with the financial burden, but his fears were unwarranted since Graham and Victor had money enough to purchase items from the estate sale.[297]

On November 4, 1844, James Polk, a Democrat, won the presidency over the Whig candidate, Henry Clay. Bennett Abell did not vote since three days before the election he had gone back to Kentucky for another estate sale at Lashfield. He bought a number of items, including a bed. In addition to a book in Latin, he acquired William Paley's *Natural Theology; or, Evidences of the Existence and Attributes of the Deity*, a book that Lincoln also owned. He also purchased the *Columbia Orator*, a volume consisting of debates on controversial topics, among them the dispute over slavery.[298]

Nathaniel Owens's twenty slaves were appraised and priced according to their health and to the work they could do for their new owners. A female slave's value included her fertility as the bearer of children. Big Tom could be bought for $750, while Cynthia, with her twin children, cost $600. Reflecting the economics of slavery in Kentucky during the 1840s, the Owens slaves were not sold but rented since it was cheaper in the short run.[299]

Assuming these slaves had been at Lashfield for a number of years, Elizabeth Abell would have known them by name. Rachel might have been a playmate around the house. And in the prime of life, York had tended the fields of tobacco plants. If there was one aspect of slavery that was humane, slave owners, unlike northern factory owners, fed and sheltered those who were too ill or old to work. Rachel, York, Mary and an old superintendent had no value.[300]

On his trips to and from Lashfield, Bennett Abell traveled through the region, where his older brother, Robert A. Abell, had a parish. The priest had been vice-president of St. Joseph's College in Bardstown until being put in charge of the congregation at New Haven in the fall of 1844. After helping to erect the church of St. Catherine, he remained at the parish until 1860. Some twenty miles north of Lashfield, New Haven was down the Bardstown Road from St. Thomas, where the brothers had attended the seminary and their mother was buried. They had not seen each other since Bennett Abell's move to Illinois. There would have been much to talk about between the apostate and the priest. While one brother had fled from the church and Kentucky slavery, the other had remained devoted to faith and tradition.[301]

IV

A Whig convention met in Petersburg on May 2, 1846, and nominated Lincoln for congressman. His platform ignored the border crisis with Mexico and the disagreement with Britain over the control of Oregon Country. Nine days later, President Polk sent his war message to Congress because Mexico had attacked U.S. troops in the disputed region. Congress declared war on Mexico after a two-day debate. Lincoln and his opponent, Peter Cartwright, supported the war. Lincoln soon took the

Sam Hill built the New Salem Carding Mill and Wool House in 1835. Two oxen walking on a slanted wheel supplied the power. The Bales bought the mill in 1837 and moved it to Petersburg in the 1840s. Bennett Abell and other farmers raised sheep for personal needs and to supplement their income. They paid either cash for the carding or a share of the wool. Another work project of President Franklin Roosevelt's New Deal, the Civil Conservation Corps constructed a replica of the mill in the 1930s. *Author's collection.*

extreme position on Oregon Country by favoring annexation of the entire region. Cartwright, a Methodist minister, charged Lincoln with religious infidelity. The campaign, however, came down to party organization and personal popularity. In this respect, Lincoln had the advantage, and his victory in the August election turned out to be overwhelming. Under the practice of the times, Lincoln would not take office for more than a year. He continued to practice law in Springfield and before the U.S. Eighth District Court.

During the campaign, Bennett Abell had been charged with nonfeasance and neglect of duty as a supervisor for Menard County. Along with three other indicted supervisors, he retained Lincoln as defense counsel. Back in March 1846, the Menard County commissioners appointed him road supervisor for district two. All persons in the county were "liable by law to perform road labor [and] be required to work two days each on some public road in the County, and that a tax of ten cents on every 100 dollars worth of real Estate on the assessment of 1846 be levied for road purposes."[302]

Bennett Abell had the responsibility of making sure these orders were carried out in the region located just south of Petersburg and bordering on the east by the Sangamon River. The district consisted of a region over ten square miles in area. Near the northeastern corner of the district, the Abell farm ran west from the river, crossing the Springfield–Petersburg Road and ending beyond the bluff that overlooked his fields. When the winter months had left the roads and bridges in their worst condition, he had the thankless job of policing the farmers in the district, who like himself were busy with the spring plowing and planting.

Before the Menard County Circuit Court in June, the grand jury announced the charges against Bennett Abell and the other defendants:

> Bennett Abel [sic] did not keep in good repair, safe & usable a certain bridge across a drain near Bales Mill on the road leading from Petersburg in Menard County to Springfield...[and] it became dangerous to travelers to cross...[He] did not keep in good repair, smooth & unobstructed that part of the...said road which runs on

the west side of A.H. Goodpastures field & to become out of repair, rough & obstructed with stumps, holes & ruts & did not cause the stumps to be leveled so as to afford a free and safe passage to wagons & carriages…On motion of the Attorney General pro tem, [the judge ordered each case] *returnable to the next term of this court, to which term said cases are continued, and that the clerk endorse an order…requiring the Sheriff to hold each Defendant to bail in the sum of one hundred dollars.*[303]

On September 2, 1846, Sheriff Amberry Rankin received an order "to take Bennett Abell, if he shall be found in your county, and him safely keep, so that you may have his body before the Circuit Court of said county on the first day of the next term thereof to be held at the court house in Petersburg."[304] Some two months later, Rankin endorsed bail that had been provided by C.G. Brooks. Perhaps the time delay can be explained by the fact that Abell lived only a mile from the sheriff's office, and he was certainly not a hardened criminal. Rankin also knew that Abell had voted for him in 1844.[305] Until making bail, however, Abell could have been legally incarcerated at any time. But Rankin had waited until four days before the trial to enforce the $100 bail ordered by the court.

At the November term of the circuit court, which actually met in early December, Bennett Abell sat beside Lincoln in the Petersburg courthouse. Typical of courthouses around the circuit, the utilitarian building had whitewashed walls, unpainted woodwork, pine floors and wooden benches. A large Franklin stove heated the room "with yards of stovepipe running wildly through the air, searching for an exit, and threatening momentarily to unjoint and tumble in sections."[306]

Bennett Abell was the first of the supervisors to go on trial, but of the three witnesses giving evidence against him, only Dr. L.G. Rogers came to court that morning. A subpoena bearing the names of the witnesses had been sent to Sheriff Rankin in November, but Robert Bishop and Ossian Ross had not been served. The records do not show any details of the proceedings, but with only one witness in the courtroom, Lincoln probably made a motion to have the charges dropped since no corroborating testimony could prove Abell guilty of nonfeasance. The official ruling was *nolle prosequi*, and the court clerk recorded the following on Wednesday, December 2, 1846: "This day came the attorney general pro tem [David Logan] and says he will not further prosecute him [Bennett Abell]. It is there fore ordered by the court that the defendant be discharged & that he go hence without delay."[307] Lincoln successfully defended the other three supervisors as well.

8

GRAHAM
Hard Times

I

In the 1840s, Mentor Graham taught at numerous schools, including Salem, Pleasant Hill, Indian Point, Walnut Ridge, Hickory Grove and Hog Corner. From 1846 to 1855, he held classes at three different schools each term. While farming and teaching, Graham supplemented his income doing construction work for the county and received $275 for building a jail in June 1843.[308] He lost an election for Menard County clerk, which would have helped financially. Graham also made extra money peddling books around the county, but his need for money soon led him to borrowing from his friends and neighbors.[309]

Lucy Robertson of Tallula recalled a visit from Mentor Graham hoping to sell books to her parents. Lucy took his hat, as she had been taught, and offered him a seat. While waiting for her parents, little conversation ensued because of Lucy's shyness. Asking the hour, Graham discovered she did not know how to tell time on a clock. "So he stood me before the Seth Thomas clock—which I still have, and explained it over and over to me. When we saw my parents coming, he said: 'Now you surprise them. Tell them what time it is when they come in.' It was a memorable day…I remember going around for days bragging to my older brothers and sisters who did not know how."[310]

In October 1844, Graham borrowed $100 from Nancy Green, and John Y. Owens, a cousin, consigned the note. (An executor of his father's

James Rutledge built a cabin for his home in 1828 and then decided to use it as a tavern for travelers. Nelson Alley bought and rented the tavern in 1833. Four years later, Jacob Bale purchased the property for his residence. In addition to the carding mill, he also owned the saw- and gristmill. Mentor Graham taught Jacob's children from 1833 to 1840. The building had wasted away into history by the 1880s. The State of Illinois built a replica of the tavern in 1936. *Author's collection.*

estate, Owens was in Illinois to collect old debts owed to Nathaniel Owens. A few days later, Bennett Abell left for Kentucky with him.) Graham promised to repay the loan in a year at 12 percent interest but defaulted, and Green sought the help of Lincoln to collect the money. Lincoln and his new law partner, William H. Herndon, filed the lawsuit on November 4, 1845, in the Menard County Circuit Court. "Nancy Green plaintiff," Lincoln wrote, "complains of Mentor Graham, defendant, in custody… (although often requested) has not…paid the said sum of money in said note specified…[And] has wholly neglected and refused and still does neglect and refuse to make payment to the plaintiff."[311]

After a brief trial, the court clerk recorded the decision of the judge: "This day came the Plaintiff by Lincoln and Herndon her attorneys and the said Defendant in proper person comes and confesses…It is therefore considered and adjudged by the court that the Plaintiff recovers of the

Defendant the said sum of one hundred and twelve dollars and twenty three cents." In addition, Graham had to pay her lawyer fees and court costs. The judgment could have been worse since Nancy Green had wanted damages that would have required him to pay her a total of $200.[312]

Regardless of the amount, Graham still had to find a way to come up with the money or face a sheriff's sale of his property. Paying an old debt from his New Salem days, Lincoln gave him a bill for $10 that Jacob Bale owed for work done back in 1834. Graham then produced documents, which were admitted into court, proving the same Jacob Bale owed him over $100 for teaching the Bale children from 1833 to 1840. Besides owning the mill on the Sangamon River, the Bale family had purchased the site of the now-deserted New Salem village. Bale had little choice except to pay his old debts or face the same legal action and costs.[313]

On South Shore Road, a sign welcomes campers to attend church in Mentor Graham's New Salem Schoolhouse. The site of Graham's farm is half a mile to the southwest. During the Civil War, Graham stopped attending meetings of the Intellectual Improvement Association because he believed most of the members were disloyal to the Union. The group met next to Graham's farm at S.D. Masters's home; the road leading to his neighbor became known as Secesh Lane. A native of Tennessee, Masters was the grandfather of Edgar Lee Masters. *Author's collection.*

In the meantime, Mentor Graham endured the frustrations of teaching the community's feisty children. Edgar Lee Masters heard that Graham was "the subject of practical jokes. My father, who was full of pranks, lowered a tin bug in front of his face, standing behind him. He struck at the bug and my father lifted it, then lowered it again when Graham again struck at it. He finally said querulously, 'Did any of you by possibility notice a bug in front of my face?' So he was precise to the end."[314]

Only a boy at the time, Masters remembered Graham walking the streets of Petersburg, "a testy and irritable old man." However, Masters had been told of the younger man. "Perhaps Mentor Graham goes down in American annals as one of its memorable schoolteachers. He is in all the books on Lincoln, and one of [Vachel] Lindsay's last poems was about him." Masters also heard that Graham "was much in the courts, suing or being sued. Before my day, on one occasion he was sued by Mrs. Bowling Green, the widow of the justice of the peace at New Salem. Another time in a suit which his son was involved he convulsed the courtroom by his snappy answers to questions and by his visible distaste for the proceedings."[315]

II

Lincoln opposed Mentor Graham in another case during that same November session. *People v. Pond* concerned the Underground Railroad in Menard County. Part of the route ran from Farmington (Farmingdale today) to Petersburg. Many of the settlers from Kentucky opposed those who helped fugitive slaves. Samuel and Marvin Pond were often seen driving a tarpaulin-covered wagon, assumingly with a cargo of produce, along with all the other traffic on the busy road that skirted the Sangamon River. Originally from Camden, New York, the brothers lived in Greenview about eight miles from the Abell farm. A neighbor from Vermont, Asa Cleaveland, lived on a farm known as Yankee Hill, suspected of being a station on the Underground Railroad for runaways from Missouri and Kentucky.[316]

On June 17, 1845, Sheriff Rankin of Menard County placed a notice in the newspaper about a fugitive slave apprehended in Petersburg: "[A] negro man deemed to be a runaway slave. Said negro is about thirty years of age, five feet two or three high, is quite dark complected [*sic*], very effeminate voice, supposed to have been a house boy. Had on him when taken up a blue frock coat, janes pantaloons and Valenita [*sic*] vest. Says his master lives in Kentucky, about five miles from Lexington, and his name is Wm [*sic*] Hanley. The owner is requested to come and prove property, pay charges and take him away."[317]

A grand jury met for its June term of the Menard County Circuit Court and indicted Marvin B. Pond because he "did unlawfully harbor a negro slave called John Hanley, the said negro slave then & there owing service and labor to one William Hanley in the State of Kentucky and the said negro slave then and there being a fugitive escaping from said service…Contrary to the form of the statute in such case…against the peace & dignity of the name of the People of the State of Illinois."[318] Representing Pond, Lincoln was able to delay the trial until the next court term, and the defendant was released on bail after his brother posted a bond of $300. Although claiming to be opposed to slavery, Mentor Graham happened to be one of four witnesses who testified against Pond. He believed the law had to be upheld. Graham's family had split over slavery since two brothers owned slaves in Kentucky.[319]

In late October, Sheriff Rankin and his deputy rode out to the witnesses' farms and "served by reading to all within named" the court's summons. Mentor Graham and the others were told "personally to be and appear before the circuit court of said county on the first day of the next term… and the truth to speak on the part of…the People of the State of Illinois [who] are plaintiff and Marvin B. Pond [who] is defendant, and this they shall in no wise on it under the penalty of the law."[320] Even if Graham had second thoughts of again testifying against Pond, he had no choice but to appear in court and tell the truth.

On November 3, Lincoln bought a pair of dollar suspenders at Irwin's store before riding out of Springfield and taking the road for Petersburg.[321] As usual, the courthouse would have been packed with spectators. Lincoln and Herndon sat with Pond across from the prosecutor, David B. Campbell, attorney general pro tem for the state of Illinois. Samuel H.

Treat, associate justice of the Illinois Supreme Court, presided and ruled that "the defendant by his attorney moves to quash the second count in the indictment, which motion being heard it is ordered that the same be sustained and for plea to the first count, in the indictment, the defendant says he is not guilty as charged there in, and for his trial puts himself on the country, and the People do the like."[322]

After the state presented its case, Lincoln argued that Mentor Graham and the other witnesses had given the wrong name when informing on his client. They had confused him with his brother, Samuel S. Pond. At the same time, there was insufficient evidence.[323] When the defense rested and the jurors had deliberated, the clerk recorded the verdict: "We of the jury find the Defendant Not Guilty in manner and form as he is charged in the indictment. It is therefore ordered that said defendant be discharged and that he go hence without delay."[324] Lincoln and Herndon were paid five dollars for their legal work, and William Hanley of Kentucky reclaimed ownership of his slave using the powers granted him by the Fugitive Slave Law of 1793. Decades earlier, Nathaniel Owens had used the same act to retrieve a slave named Bob who had fled to Pennsylvania.[325]

Curiously, on March 6, 1848, Mentor Graham did not vote the day Illinois' new constitution gained approval by the voters. In a separate balloting, Article XIV directed the legislature to "pass such laws as will effectively prohibit free persons of color from immigrating to and settling in this state; and to effectively prevent the owners from bringing them into this state for the purpose of setting them free." In the Menard County Courthouse, Petersburg precinct matched the approval percentage of the state's voters. Mentor Graham's father, Jeremiah Graham, along with Bennett Abell, voted for the constitution and the article.[326]

Central Illinois continued to have a southern bias supporting slavery. Nevertheless, more people began to arrive from northern states and Europe opposing slavery. Sung to the melody of "America," a popular song echoed their opposition to the majority of the population, who feared emancipation:

My country 'tis of thee,
Dark land of slavery,
For thee I weep.
Land where the slave has sighed,
Land where he toiled and died
To serve a tyrant's pride,
For thee I weep.[327]

Teaching during the Civil War, Mentor Graham had problems with the children of
Copperheads, many of whom did not attend classes but harassed him outside the
schoolhouse. He taught for the last time in 1878 at Liberty School in Menard County.
Graham died in 1886 while living with his son in South Dakota. In 1933, Mary Graham
had her grandfather's remains reburied next to his wife's grave in Farmers' Point Cemetery,
a few miles south of New Salem State Historic Site. The Illinois State Historical Society
erected a marker in 1955, calling him the teacher of Abraham Lincoln. *Author's collection.*

9

ABELL

Clouds without Sunshine

I

Elizabeth Abell first heard about the death of her brother, Sam Owens, on May 6, 1847. The *Sangamo Journal* reported details of the battle in the Mexican War: "Battle of Chihuahua—The Mexican force 4,223—American 924—Death of Col. Samuel C. Owens—300 Mexicans killed—Two Americans killed and seven wounded. Col. Samuel C. Owens of Independence [Missouri], who was in action as a major of the volunteer traders, was the only one killed upon the field."[328]

Within a matter of weeks, Illinois troops returned home from the hardships of combat in Mexico. Thousands of people celebrated the Fourth of July by honoring the veterans in Springfield. Colonel John J. Hardin had been killed in action, and the soldiers of the First Illinois Regiment brought the body of their commander home for burial in Jacksonville.

Congressman Lincoln spoke to a crowd in Petersburg on October 23, 1848. In the House of Representatives, he had criticized the Mexican War with his Spot Resolutions. The *Register*, a Democratic paper, reported that "Lincoln attempted…to make a defense of his course in Congress… [and] beat a retreat to Springfield."[329] Lincoln claimed President Polk had brought on a war that was unconstitutional and unnecessary. Perhaps, Bennett Abell saw the resolution as politicking and did not feel that

Lincoln had failed to support those who had fought and died in Mexico. The Whigs wanted the Democrats out of the White House, and the end justified the means.

During the presidential campaigns, both major parties attempted to reconcile northern and southern difference over the spread of slavery into the land ceded by Mexico. Lewis Cass, the Democratic candidate from Michigan, supported popular sovereignty. He believed the settlers in a territory should decide the question of slavery. Zachary Taylor, a resident of Louisiana and the owner of one hundred slaves, did not have an official platform because the Whig Party was divided in the North and South over the controversy. Taylor ran as a hero of the Mexican War and avoided taking a stand on the issue of slavery, promising to use only veto power to enforce the Constitution. Only former president Martin Van Buren of the Free-Soil Party took the stand that opposed any more slave states.[330]

On November 7, 1848, the election took place in Petersburg's Menard County Courthouse. Laura Nance remembered the excitement of election days in Menard County:

Elections and apples always belonged together for me. We made doughnuts on election day and in the evening brought up bowls of cool, crisp apples from the cellar. Neighbors and relatives, usually of the same political party, gathered as we waited for the returns which were brought by horseback in the early times and sent on to a neighbor in the same way... The apple and doughnut bowls were filled several times, the cider jug also whose contents were more or less potent, according to what the weather had been. The barrel of cider lying on its side had been out on the north side of the smoke house since apple cutting time. If the weather had been freezing for several days, you know what froze to the outside of the barrel and what came out of the spigot from the center of into the cider jug.[331]

Bennett Abell voted for the nine Whig electors supporting Taylor for the presidency. At the end of the day, the votes were counted and certified by the election judges of the precinct: Cass defeated Taylor 164 to 116 votes, while Van Buren did not receive a single vote.[332] Cass won the electoral votes of Illinois but lost the national election to Taylor. Like the Liberty Party in 1844, the Free-Soil Party captured enough votes in New York to determine which major party won the presidency.

The following spring, the discovery of gold in California caused a sensation in Menard County. "Like a contagious fever or the breaking out of war," Laura Nance recalled, "there began a hurried mobilization of our brothers and the sons of neighbors, the very cream of the young men from all directions." Dr. I.G. Rogers joined those leaving with dreams of striking it rich in California. Mike Whitlinger borrowed $500 to pay for the expense of the journey. "The early settlers who had come west with their families of small children…now began to equip grown sons, sometimes young husbands for the gold fields far beyond the Rocky Mountains, 3,000 miles away."[333]

John Abell, eldest of the Abell children, had left home after marrying the daughter of Bowling and Nancy Green in 1846. He arranged for

John Abell was the eldest son of Bennett and Elizabeth Abell. In his youth, he carried Lincoln's measuring chain during surveys. Abell married the daughter of Bowling and Nancy Green and then left her with his parents while he sought his fortune in the California gold rush. She died without seeing him again. In the late 1850s, Abell went to San Antonio, Texas, and then to Saltillo, Mexico, where he met Juana Siller, the daughter of a German Spanish family. They were married in a Catholic ceremony on January 15, 1860. *Lea Thomas collection.*

his wife to live with his parents. According to Bennett Abell, his son "furnished his wife with money and property enough…to keep…[Lizzie] in a genteel comfort style according to her desire and fashion." Then one day, she surprised Bennett Abell, leaving his "house without cause" to live next door with her mother.[334]

The California gold rush soon led the nation into a crisis with the threat of disunion on the horizon. The territory applied for statehood with a constitution prohibiting slavery. If approved, the slave states would become a minority in the Senate like they already were in the House of Representatives.

Senator Stephen A. Douglas of Illinois played a major role in what became known as the Compromise of 1850. After the death of Taylor, who had opposed some aspects of the compromise, Millard Fillmore, the new president, supported Henry Clay's resolutions. Douglas worked with Clay to organize support for the separate bills that were passed by Congress and signed by Fillmore in September.

As a result, California became a free state, while New Mexico and Utah Territories had no restrictions on slavery. Texas was reduced in size in exchange for its debt being paid by the federal government. An amendment to the Fugitive Slave Law gave the courts greater powers to arrest and return runaways. Finally, the slave trade, but not slavery, ended in the District of Columbia. In reality, moderate Democrats like Douglas were more responsible than the Whigs for the compromise that delayed disunion and war until the end of the decade.

While Congress debated the fate of the Union, everyday life went on for the people of Menard County. On May 25, 1850, Bennett Abell endorsed a new plow in the *Daily Journal*: "I certify that I have had nearly all kinds of plows on my farm—having followed plowing for many years, and of all the plows I have ever seen used. I say emphatically, that the Occidental is far superior to any. Any man can see at a glance that it possesses all the requisites necessary to make it last much longer than any other. I therefore cheerfully recommend this plow to the public."[335]

On the same day of the advertisement, the weather had been unseasonably warm. About suppertime, a high wind suddenly brought a cold rain that came down in torrents. Then hail, some larger than hens' eggs, began to fall and accumulated to a depth of a foot or more. Farmers had no time to bring in the livestock, resulting in the death of helpless calves, hogs and chickens. Birds, rabbits and other wildlife also suffered. The hail cut down and flattened crops. Defoliated trees looked as though it were late autumn.[336]

Six miles from the Abells, a man by the name of Leach was caught in the storm near his farm in Greenview. Riding his horse with no shelter in sight, Leach quickly "dismounted and ungirthing the saddle he put it over his head as a helmet…Now and then a stone of unusual size would strike the saddle with such force as to stagger him and cause him to see whole constellations of stars." Creeks flooded their banks, and hailstones piled up into ice mounds that took weeks to melt. On the Fourth of July, celebrants drank ice water at Independence Day picnics. "True, the crops were ruined and the prospect for the coming winter was a little dark, but what good would foreboding and repining do?"[337]

II

The first Menard County fair took place in the summer of 1851. Fairgoers riding in wagons and on horses passed the Abell farm, heading for the biggest event of the season in Petersburg:

> Colonel J.W. Judy was the ring marshal. For several years following, the fair was held in the hollow known as Hemp Factory Hollow… [and in] a long building used for the preparation of hemp for factory use…A great deal of hemp was grown around here. This building was used during the fair for exhibiting farm products, cookery, and needle work. The lower ground below the building was used as a show ring. The hill served as seats.[338]

Community events in Menard County usually included a fish fry prepared in a shed on the fairgrounds. "With a boy to feed the fire as he directed, the fish-frying chef was ready for his work. The fish, were cleaned, scraped and cut into quarter-pound sections…He emptied a sack of salt upon two bushels of meal…[and] spread two pounds of pepper over the meal and the salt…[then] thoroughly mixed the mess, and stirred the pieces of fish…In the long string of pans the lard was beginning to smoke when the master [chef] threw in the fish." Outside, a hungry crowd stood in line behind a rope, and they "were handed the loaves of bread and the hot fried fish in countless wooded plates, hour after hour."[339]

Meanwhile, Nancy Green had other matters on her mind that summer. On August 30, she filed suit against John Abell to collect $318, "being for needs of his said [late] wife Elizabeth Abell, including her washing & for period of near five years for cash paid on account of the wife of said Abell in bills for necessaries at merchants—physician bills and expenses attending the last sickness and the death of his said wife including her funeral expenses."[340] Bennett Abell retained William H. Herndon to represent his son, who had gone to California. "Green attached [John] Abell's Menard County property…[He] defaulted and a jury awarded $304 to Green. The court also garnished $280.50 that [Alexander] Pemberton and Felix Green[e] owed [John] Abell to help pay the judgment."[341]

After considering a move for a number of years, Bennett and Elizabeth Abell sold their farm in the early 1850s and went to Blandinsville Township in McDonough County, Illinois.[342] Robert Conover of Tallula, Illinois, bought the farm. A former justice of the peace, Conover was from Green County, Kentucky. His father-in-law, Enos Osburn of Rock Creek, Illinois, a Virginian-born Democrat, sympathized with the South during the Civil War.[343]

III

During his campaign for the Senate in 1858, Lincoln challenged the incumbent, Stephen Douglas, to a series of debates. Since the subject matter concerned the entire nation, Lincoln became nationally known due to the newspaper coverage. A Democrat favoring states' rights, Douglas had authored the Kansas-Nebraska Act of 1854, which opened the two territories to slavery depending on the choice of the settlers. What could not be decided by peaceful elections soon led to violence in Kansas. The legislation split the Whig Party, and the northern faction founded the Republican Party. Lincoln, now a Republican, opposed any more slave states entering the Union.

At Freeport, Illinois, in August, Lincoln asked Douglas how he could reconcile popular sovereignty with the Supreme Court's recent decision in the Dred Scott case that Congress could not deprive slave owners of their property without due process of law. Douglas answered "that slavery cannot exist a day or an hour, unless it is supported by local police regulations." Douglas would win the election but in the end angered the South with his so-called Freeport Doctrine and doomed his chances of southern Democrats supporting him for the presidency in 1860. Near the conclusion of the campaign in late October, Lincoln passed through Blandinsville and visited with Bennett Abell.[344]

In the late summer and early autumn of 1858, Lincoln debated and campaigned against Stephen Douglas for the U.S. Senate. Lincoln stopped in Blandinsville, Illinois, on October 24, 1858. He met with a close friend from his New Salem days and gave him an ambrotype with a salutation: "To Bennett Abell from his old friend, A. Lincoln." The omission of Elizabeth Abell's name remains a mystery. Mrs. Irene Buckles inherited the picture from her mother, Lizzie (Abell) Babbitt. *Courtesy of Ben Roth.*

A year later, Lincoln went to Kansas, keeping a promise to Republican friends that he would speak in the smoldering territory. He arrived by railroad in St. Joseph, Missouri, on December 1. The bitter cold weather froze over the Missouri River. At the Hannibal Station, he gave a short speech and then crossed the river to Elwood. He spoke in the Great Western Hotel dining room. According to the *Elwood Free Press*, Lincoln's talk focused on why the word "slave" was not mentioned in the Constitution: "The Framers of the Organic Law believed that the Constitution would outlast Slavery and they did not want a word there to tell future generations that Slavery had ever been legal in America." On the subject of Bleeding Kansas, he said, "There had been strife and bloodshed here; both parties had been guilty of outrages."[345]

The following day, Lincoln talked in Troy, Doniphan and Atchison, where he met Bennett Abell's cousin, Colonel Peter T. Abell, a supporter of slavery in Kansas. They had a cordial visit talking about Kentucky relatives and friends. On December 3, Lincoln reached Leavenworth, only five miles across the river from Jesse and Mary Vineyard's farm in Platte County, Missouri. His brother, John Vineyard, along with Colonel Abell and other proslavery Missourians, had formed the Platte County Self-Defensive Association or Blue Lodge in 1854.[346] They were determined that Kansas Territory would become a slave state and resolved to expel all settlers sent by northern abolitionists. Election fraud and intimidation soon led to violence on both banks of the Missouri River.

On November 29, 1854, in Leavenworth, an election had taken place in George H. Keller's home: "I think there were 100 or 200 persons from Missouri...Mr. Jesse Vineyard told me their determination to come here and vote on all occasions...[T]hey intended to come over here and stay long enough to vote at any rate, and make this a slave State at all hazards."[347] At the end of March 1855, Blue Lodgers were openly armed as they gathered in Weston for another election in Kansas. All had tufts of hemp, the symbol of Platte County, in their buttonholes and hats. On a long pole, a squawking goose hung by its feet. With a band playing, they headed for the dock on the Missouri River. Jesse and John Vineyard accompanied their brothers-in-law, A.G. Williams, W.A. Newman and W.E. Cunningham.[348]

By the time of Lincoln's visit, the violence had abated, but guerrilla warfare soon broke out during the Civil War. His speech in Leavenworth made reference to the hostile atmosphere of the region and John Brown's execution because of his raid on Harpers Ferry, Virginia:

> *If I might advise my Republican friends here, I would say to them, leave your Missouri neighbors alone…Drop past differences, and so conduct yourselves that if you cannot be at peace with them, the fault shall be wholly theirs…Your [South's] own statement of it is, that if the Black Republicans elect a President, you won't stand it. You will break up the Union…So, if constitutionally we elect a President, and therefore you undertake to destroy the Union, it will be our duty to deal with you as old John Brown was dealt with.*[349]

Lincoln had been staying in the home of Mark Delahay, a fellow Republican. Before departing for Springfield, he wrote an inscription in the album of Delahay's daughter. Perhaps he thought of another Mary, twenty-two years earlier, in New Salem: "Dear Mary: With pleasure I write my name in your Album. Ere long some younger man will be more happy to confer his name upon you. Don't allow it, Mary, until fully assured that he is worthy of the happiness. Dec. 7, 1859 Your friend, A. Lincoln."[350]

From late winter to early spring of 1860, Lincoln continued his campaign for the presidency in the Northeast and Midwest. The Republican National Convention in Chicago nominated him on May 18. Following tradition, he remained in Springfield while the Republicans campaigned for him. In November, he won the election against Stephen A. Douglas (Northern Democrat), John C. Breckenridge (Southern Democrat) and John Bell (Union Party). Lincoln lost to Douglas in Menard and Sangamon Counties but did well in northern Illinois, winning the state's electoral votes. Starting in late December, Southern states began to secede from the Union.

In early April 1861, Lincoln sat in his White House office, trying to focus on the Fort Sumter crisis. In the lobby, Oliver G. Abell handed a letter to an usher. At nine o'clock that morning, after eating breakfast, Lincoln started to see the job seekers and others asking favors. A secretary handed Abell's letter to Lincoln:

D.C. April 1861
His Exc [sic]
A Lincoln
Pres. U.S.A
I am here by request of my friends, relying as you can see from my paper almost solely upon your generosity for office and I would here suggest such as I feel competent to fill if by your favorable consideration I should get one—I shall ever humbly regard you as the benefactor of my parents—Consul (I have a brother at Honolulu) Register of public lands collector or Deputy of customs including Keeper of Light House—I do not mind the labor[, and] I want something sufficient to enable me to support my parents[.] Pleas[e] allow an interview of a few minutes suitable to convenience to confer upon the above.
With respect truly &c.
O.G. Abell[351]

Following their meeting, Lincoln wrote a memorandum to his commissioner of the General Land Office, James Edmunds: "Oliver G. Abell is an applicant for a Land-Office on the Pacific. Mr. Abell is the child of very intimate friends of mine, and I would like, if possible, to oblige him."[352] Instead of going to the West Coast, Abell stayed in the eye of the storm. He became a messenger and later a clerk in the General Land Office in Washington.[353] A week later, the Confederates fired on Fort Sumter, and Lincoln called for volunteers to put down the rebellion.

After passage of the Homestead Act in May 1862, business at the General Land Office increased dramatically, and Oliver spent the entire war in Washington. Sometime later, Lizzie Abell joined her brother for a year and worked in the Treasury Department. Her future husband, John Babbitt, served in the Union army.[354] Oliver witnessed the effects of the

John Babbitt enlisted for three years in the Fiftieth Illinois Volunteer Infantry on September 10, 1861. The regiment spent time in Missouri during November and December. The soldiers quartered in homes abandoned by Copperheads in St. Joseph, not far from Jesse and Mary Vineyard's farm in Platte County. The sons of Mentor Graham and Bill Greene also served in Illinois regiments. In April 1862, they fought alongside Babbitt in the Battle of Shiloh at Pittsburg Landing, Tennessee. Babbitt married Lizzie Abell in 1867. While living in Atchison County, Missouri, he joined Post 67 of the Grand Army of the Republic. *Lea Thomas collection.*

war on Washington, the celebration at war's end and the bereavement after Lincoln's assassination on April 15, 1865.

A week earlier in Kentucky, John Y. Owens, a brother of Elizabeth Abell and Mary Vineyard, had been drafted by the captain/provost marshal in Owensboro, but the records do not show he actually served. At the time, he lived on a farm in Leitchfield in Grayson County.[355] About the same time, his former slave, William Owens, joined the 124th United States Colored Infantry at Camp Nelson, Kentucky.[356] The African Americans performed garrison and guard duty in the state. More than likely, they helped to rebury the Union dead from the 1862 Battle of Perryville, many of whom were Illinois soldiers. The regiment mustered out of service on December 20, 1867. John Y. Owens had purchased William from the estate of his father, Nathaniel Owens.[357] In November 1844, the appraisers listed "Bill" as being eleven years old, with a value

Mary Vineyard's grave has become a tourist attraction in Pleasant Ridge Cemetery, located north of Weston, Missouri. A newer stone is inscribed, "Here Lies Mary Owens Vineyard Who Rejected Abraham Lincoln's Proposal of Marriage in 1837." Jesse Vineyard died in 1862 and is buried next to his wife. While their two sons served in the Confederate army, Union solders fought Rebel guerrillas and destroyed the property of Southern sympathizers in the region. In a letter to Parthena Hill, she vowed to never again call Mentor Graham a cousin if he voted for Lincoln's reelection in 1864. *Courtesy of Saundra (Owens) Robert.*

of $375.[358] William Owens may not have run away but was freed by his owner. He took on the surname of Owens and named his first son John. He lived in Leitchfield until his death during the first decade of the twentieth century.[359]

IV

After a session of the circuit court at the Petersburg courthouse in 1866, William H. Herndon took a sentimental hike through the region south of Petersburg:

About three-fourths of a mile below New Salem [then a ghost town], *at the foot of the main bluff, and in a hollow between two lateral bluffs, stands the house of Bolin [sic] Green, now uninhabited…and about the same distance north from Bolin Green's house, now at the foot of the bluff, stands the building the house and home once of Bennett Able [sic]…Their warm and generous hands were given to all and their house was wide open to all friends…These people lived for the time and place highly—had all they wished—were of good blood and fine manners. Each of these people loved company and had the best…I knew these people well and have enjoyed their unbounded hospitality.*[360]

In the 1920s, William E. Barton found a "few foundation stones, a few bricks from the hearth, a few bits of broken crockery, [which] show that once a house stood there…a frame building, eighteen by twenty feet, the home of Bennett Able [*sic*]. The visitor stands for a few

Edgar Lee Masters's childhood home is today a museum in Petersburg. He became an attorney like his father, Hardin W. Masters, and practiced law with Clarence Darrow before forming his own law firm. Nevertheless, he decided to pursue a literary career. His most admired work, *Spoon River Anthology*, is a collection of poems about the dead inhabitants of Petersburg and nearby Lewistown. A lifelong Democrat, he wrote a biography of Lincoln in 1931, portraying him as a ruthless politician who blundered the nation into war. Masters later praised New Salem's restoration and the settlers who had nurtured the young Lincoln. *Author's collection.*

minutes lost in meditation."[361] A decade later, Ida L. Bale said, "The Able [sic] home was northwest of the Green residence near the top of a high hill. Traces of the old road can still be seen after the wash of a hundred years…The Able home was replaced by a house [rebuilt by Bennett Abell] at the foot of the hill and this one by a new house constructed not many years ago."[362]

The bottomland west of the Sangamon River is still being farmed today, as it first was when Bennett Abell plowed the virgin soil over 180 years ago. Near the site of the Abell cabin, a white farmhouse is shaded by trees, and across a groomed lawn, freshly painted outbuildings glimmer brightly in the afternoon sun. The terrain beyond the bluff has changed dramatically with the construction of an earthen dam that holds the waters of Lake Petersburg. Perhaps tracing the original one, a road goes up to a housing development surrounding the lake, cutting through the forty acres that Abell bought in 1835. Looking down from the hill across the cultivated fields to the river, the view has hardly changed at all except for the utility poles and asphalt pavement of Illinois Route 97. Beyond the trees on the horizon, the vast farms of the prairie stretch endlessly to the west.

NOTES

CHAPTER 1

1. Harding, *George Rogers Clark*, 80–82.
2. Clements, *Origins of Clements-Spalding*, 80. Since Robert Abell was listed as a taxpayer in July 1788, Clements's year for Abell's departure is incorrect. Schroder and Schroeder, *Residents of Nelson County*, 5.
3. *Nelson County Court Session Book*, 37, 66.
4. Whitney, *Lincoln, the Citizen*, 115.
5. Tax Books for Green County, 1822–1823, 1827–1829.
6. Ibid., 1830.
7. William Butler quoted in Burlingame, *Oral History of Abraham Lincoln*, 19.
8. Completed in October, the U.S. Federal Census of Kentucky for June 1, 1830, listed the Abell family of two adults and five children.
9. Webb, *Centenary of Catholicity in Kentucky*, 303.
10. Gary, *Following in Lincoln's Footsteps*, 6.
11. Fehrenbacher, *Abraham Lincoln, Speeches and Writings*, vol. II, 161.
12. Reep, Houghton and Beekman, *Lincoln and New Salem*, 10.
13. Onstot, *Pioneers of Menard and Mason Counties*, 134.
14. Duncan and Nickols, *Mentor Graham*, 120–21.
15. Atkinson, "The Year of the Deep Snow," 220.

16. Onstot, *Pioneers of Menard and Mason Counties*, 134.
17. Ibid.
18. Greene to WHH (William H. Herndon), Wilson and Davis, *Herndon's Informants*, 80.
19. William Graham Greene, interview by WHH, Wilson and Davis, *Herndon's Informants*, 17.
20. John Hanks, interview by WHH, Wilson and Davis, *Herndon's Informants*, 457.
21. Burlingame, *Oral History of Abraham Lincoln*, 19; Thomas, *Lincoln's New Salem*, 60–61.
22. Fehrenbacher, *Abraham Lincoln, Speeches and Writings*, vol. II, 163.
23. *Illustrated Atlas Map of Menard County*, 10.
24. On December 6, 1831, Nathaniel Owens paid $191.37 for the 153.1 acres in the southwestern corner of Section 25. He also purchased 80.0 acres on top of the bluff, a half mile to the southwest. Illinois Public Domain Land Tract Sales Database Website.
25. Sangamon County Poll Book, August 1, 1831.
26. Ibid.
27. Ibid.
28. Beveridge, *Abraham Lincoln*, 115.

CHAPTER 2

29. Rowland and Rowland, *Clary Genealogy*, 486.
30. Thomas, *Lincoln's New Salem*, 13.
31. Miller and Ruggles, *History of Menard and Mason Counties*, 709. Rowland and Rowland, *Clary Genealogy*, 474–75.
32. Illinois Public Domain Land Tract Sales Database Website. In June 1830, William Griggs Greene purchased 160 acres next to his farm for $200.
33. See road marker on the Archeology Walk north of the second Berry-Lincoln Store.
34. Land Tract Sales, August 1829–February 1832. Green purchased 240 acres at $1.25 per acre. Illinois Public Domain Land Tract Sales Database Website.

35. Beveridge, *Abraham Lincoln*, 137, 141; Tarbell, *Early Life of Abraham Lincoln*, 143.

36. Bale, "New Salem School," 447.

37. Thomas, *Lincoln's New Salem*, 45; Records of Predestinarian Baptist Association of Sangamon.

38. Charles Clarke quoted in Thomas, *Lincoln's New Salem*, 53.

39. Illinois State Historical Society Library.

40. William Graham Greene to WHH, Wilson and Davis, *Herndon's Informants*, 17–18.

41. William Graham Greene quoted in Thayer, *Pioneer Boy*, 231.

42. Mentor Graham, interview by WHH, Wilson and Davis, *Herndon's Informants*, 9.

43. William Graham Greene quoted in "An Awkward President in Embryo Spills Milk Over the Pants of the Future Governor," *Daily Inter Ocean*, April 23, 1881, 9. Thayer, *Pioneer Boy*, 240–41.

44. Ibid.

45. Johnson Gaines Greene, interview by WHH, Wilson and Davis, *Herndon's Informants*, 365.

46. Ibid., 370.

47. William Graham Greene, interview by WHH, Wilson and Davis, *Herndon's Informants*, 367–68.

48. Lynn McNulty Greene to WHH, Wilson and Davis, *Herndon's Informants*, 80.

49 Onstot, *Pioneers of Menard and Mason Counties*, 81.

50. Mentor Graham, interview by WHH, Wilson and Davis, *Herndon's Informants*, 370.

51. Quoted in Beveridge, *Abraham Lincoln*, 120.

52. "Independent Military Companies," 23.

53. Herndon and Weik, *Herndon's Life of Lincoln*, 76.

54. Eby, *That Disgraceful Affair*, 99–100.

55. Fehrenbacher, *Abraham Lincoln, Speeches and Writings*, vol. II, 164.

56. Database of Illinois Black Hawk War Veterans, Illinois State Archives Website.

57. Thayer, *Pioneer Boy*, 247–249.

58. Ibid.

59. Fehrenbacher, *Abraham Lincoln, Speeches and Writings*, vol. II, 164. Lincoln may have been originally elected captain on April 7, 1832,

and reelected two weeks later on the farm of Greene's father. Eby, *That Disgraceful Affair*, 108.

60. Quoted in Eby, *That Disgraceful Affair*, 106.

61. Ibid, 110–12; Thayer, *Pioneer Boy*, 252–53.

62. Fehrenbacher, *Abraham Lincoln, Speeches and Writings*, vol. I, 214.

63. William Graham Greene to WHH, Wilson and Davis, *Herndon's Informants*, 18–19.

64. Royal Clary, interview by WHH, Wilson and Davis, *Herndon's Informants*, 371–72.

65. Thayer, *Pioneer Boy*, 253.

66. William Graham Greene quoted in Burlingame, *Oral History of Abraham Lincoln*, 19.

67. Thayer, *Pioneer Boy*, 254–55.

68. Fehrenbacher, *Abraham Lincoln, Speeches and Writings*, vol. I, 1.

69. Ibid., 4.

70. William Graham Greene to WHH, Wilson and Davis, *Herndon's Informants*, 20.

71. Fehrenbacher, *Abraham Lincoln, Speeches and Writings*, vol. II, 164.

72. Thayer, *Pioneer Boy*, 258.

73. Ibid., 259–60.

74. Fehrenbacher, *Abraham Lincoln, Speeches and Writings*, vol. II, 164; Thomas, *Lincoln's New Salem*, 88.

75. William Graham Greene to WHH, Wilson and Davis, *Herndon's Informants*.

76. Herndon and Weik, *Herndon's Life of Lincoln*, 89.

77. William Graham Greene to WHH, Wilson and Davis, *Herndon's Informants*, 20.

78. Barton, *Life of Abraham Lincoln*, 486–87.

CHAPTER 3

79. J. Rowan Herndon to WHH, Wilson and Davis, *Herndon's Informants*, 69–70.

80. William Butler quoted in Burlingame, *Oral History of Abraham Lincoln*, 19.

81. Irene (Babbitt) Buckles to R. Gerald McMurtry, August 20, 1940, Lincoln Memorial University Library, Harrogate, TN.

82. William Butler quoted in Burlingame, *Oral History of Abraham Lincoln*, 19.

83. J. Rowan Herndon to WHH, Wilson and Davis, *Herndon's Informants*, 69.

84. James Taylor, interview by WHH, Wilson and Davis, *Herndon's Informants*, 482.

85. J. Rowan Herndon to WHH, Wilson and Davis, *Herndon's Informants*, 91.

86. Beveridge, *Abraham Lincoln*, 135.

87. Ibid.; J. Rowan Herndon to WHH, 91. Greene claimed he had loaned Lincoln books by Gibbons and Rollin. William Graham Greene to WHH, 21; *Lincoln Lore*, "Books Lincoln Read."

88. Harvey and Heseltine, *Oxford Companion to French Literature*, 327, 365.

89. Rollin, *Ancient History of the Egyptians*, vol. II, 580.

90. Howlett, *Historical Tribute to St. Thomas' Seminary*, 13, 51.

91. Buckles to McMurtry.

92. Donald, *Lincoln*, 15.

93. Beveridge, *Abraham Lincoln*, 135; J. Rowan Herndon to WHH, Wilson and Davis, *Herndon's Informants*, 91.

94. Quoted in Wilson, *Intimate Memories of Lincoln*, 525.

95. James H. Matheny, interview by WHH, Wilson and Davis, *Herndon's Informants*, 432.

96. Ibid., 441.

97. Ibid., 557.

98. Miller, "Slaves and Southern Catholicism," 130.

99. Ibid.

100. Ibid.; Webb, *Centenary of Catholicity*, 33.

101. Miller, "Slaves and Southern Catholicism," 131.

102. *New Catholic Encyclopedia*, 17–18.

103. Clements, *Origins of Clements-Spalding*, 86.

104. Miller, "Slaves and Southern Catholicism," 131.

105. Kunhardt, Kunhardt and Kunhardt, *Lincoln, an Illustrated Biography*, 134–35.

106. Inventory Books for 1845, Green County, KY, 162–76.

107. Wolf, *Almost Chosen People*, 48.

108. Donald, *Lincoln*, 15.

109. Henry C. Whiney to WHH, Wilson and Davis, *Herndon's Informants*, 617.

110. Elizabeth Abell to WHH, Wilson and Davis, *Herndon's Informants*, 556–57.

111. Fehrenbacher, *Abraham Lincoln, Speeches and Writings*, vol. I, 19.

112. Lust, *Herb Book*, 170–71.

113. Quoted in Buley, *Old Northwest*, 257.

114. Quoted in Thomas, *Lincoln's New Salem*, 47.

115. Gore, "Early Physicians in My County," 6.

116. Berry, *Berry Patch*, 44; Spears and Barton, *Berry and Lincoln*, 98–99.

117. Buley, *Old Northwest*, 245–47, 259–60, 268.

118. Spears and Barton, *Berry and Lincoln*, 131; Berry, *Berry Patch*, 44.

119. Elizabeth Abell to WHH, Wilson and Davis, *Herndon's Informants*, 557.

120. Thomas, *Lincoln's New Salem*, 121.

121. 1850 Federal Census of Sangamon County.

122. Dr. Robert Battisti in a 1998 talk before the Cleveland Civil War Roundtable.

123. Newspaper Collection, Illinois State Historical Library.

124. Walsh, *Shadows Rise*, 76–77.

125. Sagamon County Poll Records, August 4, 1834.

126. Thomas, *Lincoln's New Salem*, 115.

127. Stevens, *Reporter's Lincoln*, 8.

128. Ibid.

129. Beveridge, *Abraham Lincoln*, 162, 164.

130. Fehrenbacher, *Abraham Lincoln, Speeches and Writings*, vol. II, 164.

131. Winkle, *Young Eagle*, 103.

132. Spears and Barton, *Berry and Lincoln*, 72.

133. Sagamon County Poll Books, August 3, 1835.

134. Ibid.

135. Spears and Barton, *Berry and Lincoln*, 74.

136. Ibid., 75.

137. Ibid.

138. Parthena Nance Hill, interview by WHH, Wilson and Davis, *Herndon's Informants*, 604–05.

139. Elizabeth Herndon Bell, interview by WHH, Wilson and Davis, *Herndon's Informants*, 605.

140. Mentor Graham, interview by WHH, Wilson and Davis, *Herndon's Informants*, 242 -243

141. William G. Greene, interview by WHH, Wilson and Davis, *Herndon's Informants*, 21.

142. Walsh, *Shadows Rise*, 76119

143. Mentor Graham, interview by WHH, Wilson and Davis, *Herndon's Informants*, 243.

144. Elizabeth Abell to WHH, Wilson and Davis, *Herndon's Informants*, 556–57.

145. Baringer and Miers, *Lincoln Day by Day*, 50.

146. Ibid., 56.

147 Fehrenbacher, *Abraham Lincoln, Speeches and Writings*, vol. I, 5-6.

148. Ibid., 6.

149. Sangamon County Poll Books, August 1, 1836.

150. On September 9, 1836, two justices of the Illinois Supreme Court granted Lincoln a license to practice law. Fehrenbacher, *Abraham Lincoln, Speeches and Writings*, vol. I, 838.

151. Sevens, *Reporter's Lincoln*, ed. Michael Burlingame, 9.

152. Fehrenbacher, *Abraham Lincoln, Speeches and Writings*, vol. I, 37.

Chapter 4

153. Nazareth Academy Enrollment Data, Spalding University Archives; Enrollment Records, Nazareth Academy Archives.

154. Spillane, *Kentucky Spring*, 144–45.

155. Howlett, *Historical Tribute to St. Thomas' Seminary*, 38.

156. Enrollment Records; Abell and Abell, 295, 299' Spillane, *Kentucky Spring*, 268.

157. Spillane, *Kentucky Spring*, 380.

158. Ibid., 131; Maraman, "Some Phases of Pioneer Education," 80.

159. Benjamin R. Vineyard to Jesse W. Weik, Wilson and Davis, *Herndon's Informants*, 610.

160. Inventory Books for 1845, 162–76.

161. Bingham, *Columbia Orator*, preface.

162. *Lincoln Lore.*

163. Pond Papers, Menard County Historical Society.

164. Ibid.

165. Ibid.

166. Ibid.

167. Ibid.

168. Kobler, *Ardent Spirits*, 62.

169. Ibid., 52, 67, 68.

170. Johnson, *Dictionary of the English Language*.

171. Pond Papers.

172. Ibid.

173. Hall, "Mary Owens Vineyard."

174. *Journal of the Illinois State Historical Society*, vol. 48, 1955: 100–01.

175. Benjamin R. Vineyard to Jesse W. Weik, Wilson and Davis, *Herndon's Informants*, 610.

176. Ibid.

177. Excerpt from a letter of Richard Blakeman in *Green County Review*, 19–20. The same story was told to the author by Kenneth Hodges, owner of the former Nathaniel Owens plantation.

178. *Journal of the Illinois State Historical Society* 48 (1955): 100–01.

179. Ibid.

180. Benjamin R. Vineyard to Jesse W. Weik, Wilson and Davis, *Herndon's Informants*, 610.

181. Thomas, *Lincoln's New Salem*, 21–22.

Chapter 5

182. Duncan and Nickols, *Mentor Graham*, 89–90; Illinois Public Domain Land Tract Sales Database website.

183. Duncan and Nickols, *Mentor Graham*, 92–93, 104.

184. Onstot, *Pioneers of Menard and Mason Counties*, 234.

185. Robert B. Rutledge to WHH, Wilson and Davis, *Herndon's Informants*, 402.

186. Mentor Graham to B.F. Irwin, quoted in Duncan and Nickols, *Mentor Graham*, 228–29.

187. Stevens, *Reporter's Lincoln*, 250.

188. Duncan and Nichols, *Mentor Graham*, 153.

189. Wolf, *Almost Chosen People*, 48; Fehrenbacher, *Abraham Lincoln, Speeches and Writings*, vol. I, 139.

190. Ibid.

191. Mentor Graham, interview by WHH, Wilson and Davis, *Herndon's Informants*, 10.

192. Interview with Greene in *Weekly Inter Ocean*, April 21, 1888.

193. Lynn McNulty Greene to WHH, Wilson and Davis, *Herndon's Informants*, 80.

194. The book is now in the Library of Congress. "L.M. Green" is written at the top of page 153. Walsh, *Shadows Rise*, 143.

195. Quoted in Walsh, *Shadows Rise*, 67.

196. Newspaper Collection.

197. Onstot, *Pioneers of Menard and Mason Counties*, 150.

198. J. Rowan Herndon to WHH, Wilson and Davis, *Herndon's Informants*, 7

199. Howard, *Life of Abraham Lincoln*, 22.

200. Duncan and Nickols, *Mentor Graham*, 161.

201. Howard, *Life of Abraham Lincoln*,

202. Thomas, *Lincoln's New Salem*, 94, 95, 100.

203. Fehrenbacher, *Abraham Lincoln, Speeches and Writings*, vol. II, 164.

204. James Miles, interview by WHH, Wilson and Davis, *Herndon's Informants*, 473

205. Fehrenbacher, *Abraham Lincoln, Speeches and Writings*, vol. II, 164–65.

206. Nelson County Court of the Quarter Sessions Book, 1791–1793, 216; Evans, *History of Green County*, 53.

207. Elizabeth Herndon Bell, interview by WHH, Wilson and Davis, *Herndon's Informants*, 606.

208. Ibid., 591.

209. Ibid.

210. Sangamon County Poll Book, November 7, 1836.

211. L.M. Greene to WHH, Wilson and Davis, *Herndon's Informants*, 250.

212. Mentor Graham, interview by WHH, Wilson and Davis, *Herndon's Informants*, 243.

213. Fehrenbacher, *Abraham Lincoln, Speeches and Writings*, vol. I, 37.

Chapter 6

214. Hertz, *Hidden Lincoln*, 259.

215. *Daily Inter Ocean*, April 23, 1881, 9.

216. Ibid.

217. Johnson Gaines Greene, interview by WHH, Wilson and Davis, *Herndon's Informants*, 530–31.

218. Baringer and Miers, *Lincoln Day by Day*, 61.

219. Johnson Gaines Greene, interview by WHHWilson and Davis, *Herndon's Informants*.

220. Ibid.

221. Fehrenbacher, *Abraham Lincoln, Speeches and Writings*, vol. I, 7.

222. Ibid.

223. Ibid., 7–8.

224. Ibid., 37–38.

225. Nicolay and Hay, *Abraham Lincoln*, 49.

226. Boone, "Rock Creek Lyceum," *Journal of the Illinois State Historical Society* 19 (1926): 69–70.

227. Pond, "New Salem Community Activities," 101.

228. Boone, "Rock Creek Lyceum."

229. Ibid., 70–71.

230. Pond, "New Salem Community Activities.".

231. Ibid., 93–96.

232. Duncan and Nickols, *Mentor Graham*, 122–23.

233. Fehrenbacher, *Abraham Lincoln, Speeches and Writings*, vol. I, 81–83, 90; Carruthers, "Abraham Lincoln's First Loves," 66.

234. New Salem Collection (SC1101), Illinois State Historical Library Manuscripts Collection.

235. Newspaper Collection.

236. Nicolay and Hay, *Abraham Lincoln*, 154.

237. Boone, "Rock Creek Lyceum," 70–71; Fehrenbacher, *Abraham Lincoln, Speeches and Writings*, vol. I, 18.

238. Burlingame, *Oral History of Abraham Lincoln*, 22.

239. Ibid., 23.

240. Fehrenbacher, *Abraham Lincoln, Speeches and Writings*, vol. I, 19.

241. Archer, *Simple Fixin's*, 11–15, 51.

242. Harriet A. Chapman to WHH, Wilson and Davis, *Herndon's Informants*, 512.

243. Mary Owens Vineyard to WHH, Wilson and Davis, *Herndon's Informants*, 262.

244. Ibid.

245. Laura Hall, daughter of Ellen (Owens) Williams, to R. Gerald McMurtry. McMurtry Papers.

246. Buckles to McMurtry.

247. Baringer and Miers, *Lincoln Day by Day*, 38–39.

248. Benjamin R. Vineyard to Jesse W. Weik.

249. Pond, "New Salem Community Activities."

250 Stevens, *Reporter's Lincoln*, ed. Burlingame, 10.

251. Baringer and Miers, *Lincoln Day by Day*, 71.

252 Fehrenbacher, *Abraham Lincoln, Speeches and Writings*, vol. I, 18-19.

253. *Lincoln Lore*, No. 446.

254. Ibid., No. 191.

255 Fehrenbacher, *Abraham Lincoln, Speeches and Writings*, vol. I, 19.

256. Ibid.

257. Ibid., 20.

258. Ibid.

259. Mary Owens Vineyard to WHH, Wilson and Davis, *Herndon's Informants*, 256.

260. Fehrenbacher, *Abraham Lincoln, Speeches and Writings*, vol. I, 39.

261. Ibid., 37–39.

262. Herndon and Weik, *Herndon's Life of Lincoln*, 125.

263. Ibid.

264. Benjamin R. Vineyard to Jesse W. Weik.

265. Ibid., 610–11.

266. Archer, *Simple Fixin's*, 14.

267. Randall, *Mary Lincoln*, 16, 43.

268. *Albert G. Williams v. John M. Cabiness, et al*, Lincoln Legal Papers.

269. Ibid.

270. Mary Owens Vineyard to WHH, Wilson and Davis, *Herndon's Informants*, 263.

271. Nancy G. Vineyard to Jesse W. Weik, Wilson and Davis, *Herndon's Informants*, 601.

272. U.S. Federal Census, 1850.

273. W.S. Davis in a letter to R. Gerald McMurtry, August 1940, McMurtry Papers.

CHAPTER 7

274. Menard County Assessor's Book, Illinois State Historical Library.

275. County Commissioners Court of Menard County, Illinois State Historical Library.

276. Onstot, *Pioneers of Menard and Mason Counties*, 74; Bale, "New Salem School," 22; Duncan and Nickols, *Mentor Graham*, 176; Henry E. Pond to R. Gerald McMurtry, "The Environs of the Lincoln-Owens Courtship," McMurtry Papers.

277. Baringer and Miers, *Lincoln Day by Day*, 190; John Bennett to WHH, Wilson and Davis, *Herndon's Informants*, 263. There are conflicting accounts about whether Lincoln spoke at both the funeral and the Masonic memorial service.

278. Whitney, *Lincoln*, 121.

279. Ibid., 141.

280. *W.L. May v. L.M. Greene and J.B. Loose*, Lincoln Legal Papers.

281. Ibid.

282. Onstot, *Pioneers of Menard and Mason Counties*, 184.

283. *Prairie Picayune*, 5.

284. *Cabot v. Regnier, Regnier v. Cabot and Torrey*, Lincoln Legal Papers; Duff, *Lincoln, Prairie Lawyer*, 90–93.

285. Fraysse, *Lincoln, Land, and Labor*, 95.

286. *Cabot v. Regnier; Regnier v. Cabot and Torrey*.

287. Ibid.

288. Baringer and Miers, *Lincoln Day by Day*, 214.

289. *Cabot v. Regnier; Regnier v. Cabot and Torrey*.

290. Ibid.

291. Ibid.; Duff, *Lincoln, Prairie Lawyer*, 90.

292. Ledgers of Dr. Francis Regnier, Illinois State Historical Library.

293. Basler, *Collective Works of Abraham Lincoln*, 310.

294. Copy of poem from John G. Owens, Lea Thomas genealogy collection.

295. Will Book 3, 73, Records of Green County, KY.

296. Allen, *History of Kentucky*, 383–84.

297. Inventory Book 7, Green County, KY. Nathaniel Owens estate totaled some $30,000, a considerable sum of money in the 1840s. The Abells' share was probably about $3,000.

298. Ibid.

299. Ibid.

300. Ibid.

301. Webb, *Centenary of Catholicity*, 500, 502.

302. *People v. Abell*, Lincoln Legal Papers.

303. Ibid.

304. Ibid.

305. Menard County Election Records, August 5, 1844.

306. Duff, *Lincoln, Prairie Lawyer*, 121.

307. *People v. Abell*.

CHAPTER 8

308. Illinois State Historical Library.

309. Duncan and Nickols, *Mentor Graham*, 254.

310. Ibid., 183–84.

311. *Green v. Graham*, Lincoln Legal Papers.

312. Ibid.

313. Duncan and Nickols, *Mentor Graham*, 185–86, 255–56.

314. Masters, *The Sangamon*, 75.

315. Ibid., 73–75.

316. Nance, *Piece of Time in Lincoln County*, 60. Laura Osburn Nance was the daughter-in-law of Thomas J. Nance.

317. *People v. Pond*, Lincoln Legal Papers.

318. Ibid.

319. Duncan and Nickols, *Mentor Graham*, 185.

320. *People v. Pond.*

321. Baringer and Miers, *Lincoln Day by Day*, 259.

322. *People v. Pond.*

323. Nance, *Piece of Time in Lincoln County*, 61.

324. *People v. Pond.*

325. Green, *Kentucky Gazette*, 59.

326. Menard County Poll Records, March 6, 1848; Duncan and Nickols, *Mentor Graham*, 187.

327. Ibid., 187.

CHAPTER 9

328. Newspaper Collection.

329. Baringer and Miers, *Lincoln Day by Day*, 323.

330. Hamilton, *Prologue to Conflict*, 9–10.

331. Nance, *Piece of Time in Lincoln County*, 60.

332. Menard County Poll Records, November 7, 1848.

333. Nance, *Piece of Time in Lincoln County*, 44, 46. Whitlinger later returned with $10,000 in gold. According to the loan agreement, he gave his creditor, Mr. Epler, $5,000.

334. *Green v. Abell*, Lincoln Legal Papers.

335. Newspaper Collection.

336. Miller and Ruggles, *History of Menard and Mason Counties*, 27.

337. Ibid., 27–28.

338. Nance, *Piece of Time in Lincoln County*, 57.

339. Stevens, *Reporter's Lincoln*, ed. Burlingame, 4–5.

340. *Green v. Abell.*

341. Ibid.

342. U.S. Federal Census, 1860.

343. Nance, *Piece of Time in Lincoln County*, 62. Enos Osburn was the author's father.

344. Irene Buckles inherited the photograph and sent a copy to R. Gerald McMurtry. "I have carefully compared your copy of my number 14 of the Lincoln ambrotype with the several copies which I have of the same ambrotype, and I think your copy is identical…It is one of the best of the early portraits." F.H. Meserve to R. Gerald McMurtry in a letter dated June 6, 1941. McMurtry Papers.

345. Ayres, *Lincoln and Kansas*, 81.

346. Paxton, *Annals of Platte County*, 184.

347. U.S. House of Representatives, "Troubles in Kansas," 30.

348. Ibid., 928.

349. Ayres, *Lincoln and Kansas*, 217–18.

350. Ibid., 130–131.

351. Lincoln Papers, Library of Congress website.

352. Basler, *Collective Works of Abraham Lincoln*.

353. Lincoln Papers.

354. Buckles to McMurtry.

355. James G. Owens's notes on his family genealogy. John Y. Owens was forty-four years old in 1865. Either his conscription was politically motivated or the story is apocryphal.

356. The Civil War, Soldiers and Sailors Database, National Park Service Website.

357. U.S. Federal Census of Green County, 1850; Grayson County, 1860; Slave Schedule of Green County, 1850.

358. Inventory Book 7, Green County, KY.

359. U.S. Federal Census of Grayson County, 1870, 1880, 1900.

360. Herndon, *Lincoln, Ann Ruthledge and the Pioneers of New Salem*, 15–17. Elizabeth Abell died in 1870, followed by Bennett Abell in 1876. They are buried in Avon, Illinois.

361. Barton, *Women Lincoln Loved*, 189.

362. Bale, *New Salem as I Knew It*, 22.

BIBLIOGRAPHY

Abell, Horace A., and Lewis P. Abell. *The Abell Family in America*. Rutland, VT: Tuttle Publishing, 1940.

Allen, William B. *History of Kentucky*. Louisville, KY, 1872.

Archer, Barbara. *Simple Fixin's: One Pot Meals and Breadstuffs from the Rutledge Tavern*. Springfield, IL: Tastes from the Past, 1999.

Atkinson, Eleanor. "The Year of the Deep Snow." In *The Prairie State, A Documentary History of Illinois, Colonial Years to 1860*. Edited by Robert P. Sutton. Grand Rapids, MN: William B. Ferdmans Publishing, Co., 1976.

Ayres, Carol Dark. *Lincoln and Kansas, Partnership for Freedom*. Manhattan, KS: Sunflower University Press, 2001.

———. "New Salem School and the Hard-Shell Church." *Journal of the Illinois State Historical Society*, vol. 40, 1947.

Bale, Ida L. *New Salem as I Knew It*. Petersburg, IL: Petersburg Observer Co., 1941.

Baringer, William E., and Earl Schenck Miers, eds. *Lincoln Day by Day, A Chronology, 1809–1865*. Vol. I. Washington, D.C.: Lincoln Sesquicentennial Commission, 1960.

Barton, William E. *The Life of Abraham Lincoln*. Indianapolis, IN: Bobbs-Merrill Co., 1925.

———. *The Women Lincoln Loved*. Indianapolis, IN: Bobbs-Merrill Co., 1927.

Basler, Roy P., ed. *The Collective Works of Abraham Lincoln*. New Brunswick, NJ: Rutgers University Press, 1953.

Berry, William. *The Berry Patch*. N.p.: self-published, 1976.

Beveridge, Albert J. *Abraham Lincoln, 1809–1858*. Vol. I. Boston: Riverside Press, 1928.

Bingham, Caleb. *The Columbia Orator*. Albany, NY: D. Farrand and Green, 1811.

Blakeman, Richard. *Green County Review*. Greensburg, KY: Green County Historical Society, 1984.

"Books Lincoln Read." In *Lincoln Lore*, no. 167. Fort Wayne, IN: Lincoln Museum.

Boone, Robert E., ed. "Rock Creek Lyceum." *Journal of the Illinois State Historical Society* 19 (1926).

Buley, R. Carlyle. *The Old Northwest, Pioneer Period, 1815–1840*. Bloomington: Indiana University Press, 1950.

Burlingame, Michael, ed. *An Oral History of Abraham Lincoln. John G. Nicolay's Interviews and Essays*. Carbondale: Southern Illinois University Press, 1996.

———. *A Reporter's Lincoln*. Lincoln: University of Nebraska Press, 1998.

Carruthers, Olive. "Abraham Lincoln's First Loves." In *Lincoln for the Ages*. Edited by Ralph G. Newman. Garden City, NY: Doubleday, 1960.

Clements, J.W.S. *Origins of Clements-Spalding and Allied Families of Maryland and Kentucky*. Louisville, KY: Standard Press, 1928.

Court of the Quarter Sessions Book, 1791–1793. Nelson County, KY.

Donald, David. *Lincoln*. New York: Touchstone, 1996.

Duff, John J.A. *Lincoln, Prairie Lawyer*. New York: Rinehart and Co., Inc., 1960.

Duncan, Kunigunde, and D.E. Nickols. *Mentor Graham: The Man Who Taught Lincoln*. Chicago: University of Chicago Press, 1944.

Eby, Cecil. *That Disgraceful Affair: The Black Hawk War*. New York: W.W. Norton and Co., 1973.

Enrollment Records. Nazareth Academy Archives, Nazareth, KY.

Evans, Kate Powell. *A History of Green County, Kentucky, 1793–1993*. Lexington, KY: American Printing Co., 1993.

Fehrenbacher, Don E., ed. *Abraham Lincoln, Speeches and Writings*. New York: Literary Classics of the U.S., Inc., 1989.

Fraysse, Oliver. *Lincoln, Land, and Labor, 1809–1860*. Urbana: University of Illinois Press, 1994.

Gary, Ralph. *Following in Lincoln's Footsteps*. New York: Carroll and Graf Publishers, 2001.

Gore, Spencer. "Early Physicians in My County." *Journal of the Illinois State Historical Society* 24 (1931).

Green, Karen Mauer. *Kentucky Gazette, 1801–1820*. Baltimore, MD: Gateway Press, 1985.

Hall, Virginia L. "Mary Owens Vineyard." Weston Historical Museum, Weston, MO. www.westonhistoricalmuseum.org.

Hamilton, Holman. *Prologue to Conflict: The Crisis and Compromise of 1850*. New York: W.W. Norton & Co., Inc., 1964.

Harding, Margery Heberling. *George Rogers Clark and His Men, Military Records, 1778–1784*. Frankfort: Kentucky Historical Society, 1981.

Harvey, Paul, and J.E. Heseltine. *The Oxford Companion to French Literature*. London: Oxford at the Clarendon Press, 1959.

Herndon, William H. *Lincoln, Ann Ruthledge and the Pioneers of New Salem*. Herrin, IL: Trovillion Private Press, 1945.

Herndon, William H., and Jesse W. Weik. *Herndon's Life of Lincoln*. New York: Da Capo Press, 1983.

Hertz, Emanuel, ed. *The Hidden Lincoln from the Letters and Papers of William H. Herndon*. New York: Viking Press, 1938.

Howard, James Q. *The Life of Abraham Lincoln with Extracts from His Speeches*. Columbus, OH: Follett, Foster, Co., 1860.

Howlett, William J. *Historical Tribute to St. Thomas' Seminary at Poplar Neck near Bardstown, Kentucky*. St. Louis: B. Herder, 1906.

Illinois Black Hawk War Veterans Database. Illinois State Archives website. http://www.cyberdriveillinois.com/departments/archives/databases/blkhawk.html.

Illinois Public Domain Land Tract Sales Database website. http://www.cyberdriveillinois.com/departments/archives/databases/data_lan.html.

Illustrated Atlas Map of Menard County, Illinois 1874. Edwardsville, IL: W.R. Brink & Co., 1874.

Inventory Books for Green County, Kentucky.

Johnson, Samuel. *A Dictionary of the English Language*. Philadelphia: Jacob, Johnson & Co., 1805.

Kobler, John. *Ardent Spirits: The Rise and Fall of Prohibition*. New York: Da Capo Press, 1993.

Kunhardt, Philip B., Jr., Philip B. Kunhardt III and Peter W. Kunhardt. *Lincoln, an Illustrated Biography*. New York: Random House, 1992.

Ledgers of Dr. Francis Regnier. Illinois State Historical Library, Springfield, IL.

The Lincoln Legal Papers. Illinois State Historical Library, Springfield, IL.

Lincoln Papers. Library of Congress website. http://www.loc.gov/index.html.

Lust, John. *The Herb Book*. New York: Bantam Books, 1974.

Maraman, Wenonah. "Some Phases of Pioneer Education on the Kentucky Frontier with Emphasis on Nelson County, 1785–1860." Master's diss., University of Louisville, 1943.

Masters, Edgar Lee. *The Sangamon*. New York: Farrar and Rinehart Inc., 1942.

McMurtry, R. Gerald Files. Lincoln Memorial University Library, Harrogate, TN.

Miller, Randall M. "Slaves and Southern Catholicism." In *Masters and Slaves in the House of the Lord*. Edited by John B. Boles. Lexington: University Press of Kentucky, 1988.

Miller, R.D., and J.M. Ruggles. *History of Menard and Mason Counties, Illinois*. Chicago: O.L. Baskin, 1879.

Nance, Laura Osburn. *A Piece of Time in Lincoln Country*. Edited by Georgia Goodwin Creager. Published by editor, 1968.

Nazareth Academy Enrollment Records. Spalding University Archives, Louisville, KY.

Nelson County Court of the Quarter Session Books. Division of Special Collections and Archives, University of Kentucky, Lexington, KY.

New Catholic Encyclopedia. New York: McGraw-Hill Book Co., 1967.

New Salem Collection. Illinois State Historical Library, Springfield, IL.

Newspaper Collection. Illinois State Historical Library, Springfield, IL.

Nicolay, John G., and John Hay. *Abraham Lincoln, A History*. Vol. I. New

York: Century Co., 1890.

Onstot, T.G. *Pioneers of Menard and Mason Counties*. Forest City, IL, 1902.

Paxton, W.M. *Annals of Platte County, Missouri*. Cape Girardeau, MO: Ramfre Press, 1965.

Pond, Fern Nance, ed. "New Salem Community Activities: Documentary." *Journal of the Illinois State Historical Society* 48 (1955).

Prairie Picayune 5, no. 6 (2000). New Salem Lincoln League, Petersburg, IL.

Randall, Ruth Painter. *Mary Lincoln, Biography of a Marriage*. Boston: Little, Brown and Co., 1953.

Records of Predestinarian Baptist Association of Sangamon, County. Illinois Historical Library, Springfield, IL.

Reep, Thomas P., C.W. Houghton and J. Colby Beekman. *Lincoln and New Salem*. Petersburg, IL: Old Salem Lincoln League, 1927.

Rollin, Charles. *The Ancient History of the Egyptians, Carthaginians, Assyrians, Babylonians, Medes and Persians, Macedonians and Grecians*. Cincinnati, OH: Applegate, 1854.

Rowland, Ralph S., and Star W. Rowland. *Clary Genealogy, Four Early American Lines and Related Families*. Sterling, VA: published by authors, 1990.

Sangamon County and Menard County Poll Books. Illinois State Archives, Springfield, IL.

Schroder, Margaret Johnston, and Carl A. Schroeder, comps. *Residents of Nelson County, Virginia (Kentucky) Recorded in Tithables and Tax Lists, 1785–1791*. Bardstown, KY: privately published, 1988.

Spears, Zarel C., and Robert S. Barton. *Berry and Lincoln, Frontier Merchants: The Store that "Winked Out."* New York: Stratford House, Inc., 1947.

Spillane, James Maria. *Kentucky Spring*. St. Meinrad, IN: Abbey Press, 1968.

Stevens, Walter B. *A Reporter's Lincoln*. St. Louis: Missouri Historical Society, 1916.

Tarbell, Ida M. *The Early Life of Abraham Lincoln*. New York: S.S. McClure, 1896.

Tax Books for Green County, KY.

Thayer, William M. *The Pioneer Boy and How He Became President*. Boston: Walker, Wise and Co., 1863.

Thomas, Benjamin P. *Lincoln's New Salem*. Carbondale: Southern

University Press, 1987.

U.S. Federal Census for Kentucky and Illinois.

U.S. House of Representatives. "Troubles in Kansas, with the Views of the Minority of Said Committee." Washington, D.C.: C. Wendell Printer, 1856.

Walsh, John Evangelist. *The Shadows Rise, Abraham Lincoln and the Ann Rutledge Legend*. Urbana: University of Illinois Press, 1993.

Webb, Ben J. *The Centenary of Catholicity in Kentucky*. Utica, KY: McDowell Publications, 1884.

Whitney, Henry C. *Lincoln: The Citizen*. New York: Current Literature Publishing Co., 1907.

Wilson, Douglas L., and Rodney O. Davis, eds. *Herndon's Informants*. Urbana: University of Illinois Press, 1998.

Wilson, Rufus Rockwell. *Intimate Memories of Lincoln*. Elmira, NY: Primaver Press, 1945.

Winkle, Kenneth J. *The Young Eagle*. Dallas, TX: Taylor Publishing Co., 2001.

Wolf, William J. *The Almost Chosen People: A Study of the Religion of Abraham Lincoln*. Garden City, NY: Doubleday and Co., 1959.

INDEX

V

Van Buren, Martin 76, 119
Vineyard, Benjamin R. 95, 139,
     140, 143
Vineyard, Jesse 98, 125
Vineyard, John 13, 86, 125
Vineyard, Mary (Owens) 98, 125, 128

W

Weston, Missouri 13, 79
Whig 46, 47, 53, 65, 76, 106, 107,
     119, 124

Y

Yates, Richard 29

ABOUT THE AUTHOR

D ale Thomas is a graduate of Kent State University (BS in social studies and education) and Case Western Reserve University (MA in history). He retired after teaching social studies for thirty-one years at Bay High School in Bay Village, Ohio. In addition to serving as a judge for History Day at Case Western Reserve University, he has been an advisor for tours at the Western Reserve Historical Society and historian for the Cleveland Civil War Roundtable.

At the present time, Thomas is the archivist and vice-president for the Olmsted Historical Society and a member of the North Olmsted Landmarks Commission. He is the author of the books *Images of America: North Olmsted* and *Then & Now: Olmsted*.

After serving in the U.S. Army, Thomas married Lea Roth in 1963. They live in North Olmsted, Ohio, and have two sons, Scot and Geoffrey. A retired teacher like her husband, Lea Thomas is a direct descendant of Bennett and Elizabeth Abell. Her interest in family genealogy led to the writing of this book.

Visit us at
www.historypress.net